THE
POLITICS
OF
INNOCENCE

D. ROBERT KENNEDY

DEDICATED

TO

the many who have suffered
from the irresponsibility of the few.

The Scripture quotations in this book are mostly from the Holy Bible New International Version, Zondervan Bible Publishers, Grand Rapids, MI. In a number of places I have paraphrased passages to integrate same with my sentence structure, but I have tried to remain faithful to the Scriptural thought.

Cover Design: Leighton Kennedy

Published by
Manchesters Publishers
East Elmhurst, New York

TO ERR IS HUMAN
TO BLAME IT UPON OTHERS
IS IRRESPONSIBLE.

CONTENTS

INTRODUCTION

It has been my view that politics inserts itself into most things we do. I do not mean party politics so much as I mean competing power play. For example, when people live to satisfy their insatiable appetites while excusing their bad attitudes and behaviors in the name of Christian compassion and personal autonomy, I call this political. To be politically correct (PC) does not mean that one is morally responsible. It might simply mean that one is afraid to speak critically of moral perversions, deviations and alternate lifestyles with sincerity. When many people are living a lie with the pretense that they are being responsible, the "Politics of Innocence" calls for a return to the bedrock of ethical values where honesty, integrity, respect for God, respect for the self and others, and personal responsibility are known.

In the context of contemporary politics there is much discussion about honesty, integrity and responsibility, but it is too often staging a political game. In confronting the general cultural situation, I fear that too many Christians are being co-opted by systems that suspend their moral and ethical judgment. They are caught in a culture too eager to assert power and too fearful to assume responsibility. When Christians endorse self-gratification, sexual perversions, deviations and alternative lifestyles, they are proclaiming the falsehood of responsibility not born of God. Thus my interest is not to attend to the public political realm as much as I intend to focus on the spiritual culture that forgets its prophetic role to speak against idolatry, immorality and injustice. While our culture runs wild with the belief that life is dictated by desire, circumstances and unlimited freedom, my interest is to ask "How can we as Christians critique the spirit of conformity and tolerance?" "How can we get ourselves to move away from the call to "cover up" and live with responsibility?" "How can we lead those who suffer with the burden of their consciences to find a new future?"

In the *Politics of Innocence* I do not just focus on a critique of moral irresponsibility but suggest the path of grace, for a true rectification of social violence and guilt will only come through the path of true repentance. By repentance I mean that we need to do an "about - face" in our behavior. And I say "our" because I follow Douglas John Hall in insisting that, "we are all personally implicated in the guilt to which we must bear witness."[1] I mean that we must not only be analyzing our society and identifying the wrong then turning with political suasion to find ways of covering the wrong to maintain a position of public favor. I also mean that we must take responsibility for the wrong and work to transform that wrong. The Sovereign Lord asked Prophet Ezekiel to raise many questions, but two are of import here namely: (1) "Do I take pleasure in the death of the wicked? (2) "Am I not pleased when they turn from their ways and live?" (Ez 18:23). These questions form the bases in my call for responsibility.

ENDNOTES

1. Douglas John Hall (1986), *Imaging God: Dominance as Stewardship*, New York: Wm. B. Eerdmans and Friendship Press, p. 23).

CHAPTER ONE

THE POLITICS OF INNOCENCE

The pretense of innocence

The political action of Pilate in washing his hands as a repudiation of his part in the condemnation and execution of Jesus (Matt 27:24-26), is a powerful lesson in moral responsibility. One might even say it is a lesson in moral irresponsibility. The action suggests one of the most blatant lack of character, courage and moral consciousness that one might ever know in history. However, it points directly to the vast number of individuals who participate in immoral deeds while blaming circumstances for their moral blindness. Many persons do not use such a dramatic gesture of handwashing for suspending their moral judgment as Pilate did, but they find some way to coverup and make it appear as if they are morally upright. But this trivialization of the sense of responsibility in contemporary society is especially conflictual since even congressional investigators are pretending a passionate sense of moral consciousness. In effect, what is needed is not political posturing, but a prophetic spirit to call for reformation. It is the prophetic spirit that calls for radical transformation of the heart. When individuals feel they can behave with mindless freedom then, like Pilate, move with a sleight of hand to get rid of all their guilt and shame, the Spirit of God must be called upon for the awakening of the soul.

I shall constantly make reference to Pilate as an archetype of immorality, though in subsidiary discussions I move beyond Pilate to focus on questions in the domain of sexuality. In the domain of sexuality we find most often that the rights of people are violated. Here we find war on the moral boundaries of life. People participate in irresponsible deeds then cast blame, appeal to excuses, and show their helplessness, more than in any other area of life. I find it important then to connect sexuality to my general interest in responsibility because in our time, sex is used as the primary access route to power, politics, popularity, and profit. There are multiple areas in which we can test the question of morality and responsibility, but today, sexuality seems to create a context where people live in moral ambiguity, where they often fail to be reflective and responsive to the spiritual impulses that call them away from brutality. My interest is to discuss responsibility, but I use sexuality as a case study of how responsible we are in our times, especially since such has become potent for discussions in the politics of morality.

Dr. Laura Schlessinger, who has done extensive work on human sexuality, says that the quality of our lives is not created solely by the events in our lives, but by the unique response we have to life.[1] H. Richard Niebuhr says the responsible person must answer to God, society and himself. If such a person fails to bring a clear interpretation to life he/she cannot be responsible.[2] William Frankena sees one sense of responsibility as one's moral sense of obligation which focuses on one's moral character. Another sense of responsibility has to do with taking responsibility for an action that is, how one responds to an action. A third understanding of responsibility has to do with whether one is faithful in something done.[3] The points emphasized in the definitions are whether one has been good, whether one has done something good, whether one has acted in the right or whether or not one has acted bad and wrong. One might say the interest is on the internal moral sense character, courage and conscience, over a merely external sense of watching action. The issue with Pilate in washing his hands was his pretense of being good while he failed to be accountable. His lack of strong resolve to do right, the weakness in his will to stand up for truth, his inclination to indulge himself, his lack of virtue allowed him to philander with principle. One can view him from the table below and see the distortions and irresponsibilities in his actions. Pilate falls to the center and right of this grid.

Responsible	Distorted	Irresponsible
Courage to act according to principle	Blaming circumstances for one's actions	Acting from fear and favor or public pressure
Making judgment from character	Blind to personal biases	Making judgment from impulsion
A clear understanding of context and consequences	Blind to context and have no care about consequences	Disregards proper procedures and consequences
Concern for community	Self-centered	Self-indulgent
Practicing honesty (Integrity)	Practicing deceit	Practicing dishonesty
Responding to life reflectively (Reason)	Acting naively	Acting irrationally
Maintaining a high moral tone - noble character	Self-gratifying	Depraved -Lacking noble character

A comparison of the life of Pilate with that of Daniel another public character, for example, makes the above points more transparent. As one commentator says, "[In Daniel's and his friends] we have an instance of the triumph of principle over temptation, of purity over depravity, of devotion and loyalty over atheism and idolatry." This commentator also states in the same reference, "True success in any line of work is not the result of chance or destiny. It is the outworking of God's providences, the reward of faith and discretion, of virtue and perseverance. Fine mental qualities and a high moral tone are not the result of accident. God gives opportunities; success depends upon the use made of them." "Pure hearts, strong hands, fearless courage, are needed; for the warfare between vice and virtue calls for ceaseless vigilance." "But only by him who determines to do right because it is right will the victory be gained."[4]

Fidelity to principles

In the temptations that come to those in high office it is easy to find infidelity in the heart, for "power corrupts and absolute power corrupts absolutely." But the model of infidelity or irresponsibility we have been discussing does not have to be maintained. There is the better understanding that the one who in high or low position, who trusts God and who depends on the divine wisdom, will be able to stand up in moments of great evil. When David committed adultery with Uriah's wife it was at a moment when his own successes had "gotten to his head." He had forgotten to be vigilant and was overcome with self-gratification and self-indulgence. In the end he committed a second most unprincipled deed by sending Uriah, the man with whose wife he had offended, to the most dangerous part of the battle. Thus Uriah was killed. When Prophet Nathan spoke to David of his deed he identified David both as an adulterer and as a murderer (2 Sam 11). It is of interest that even though David sought to hide his fault that he had done something which is forgotten by many persons of high rank today, he had humility of the heart. He did not trivialize his sin. Rienhold Niebuhr spoke often of the pride and pretensions of our age when he attacked the sensuality, the materialist interest and spiritual pride of our culture.[5] He spoke mostly of the political and social injustices which ruled the world. I submit that his idea can be applied to our times which has turned back to the Homeric days in which morality was built on erotic desires. Along with the movement to irresponsibility has come our portrayal of eroticism as the great purpose for which life is lived. Reinhold Niebuhr says that in our culture we focus on a certain part of our being to the extent that it becomes idolatrous. And then we blame our genes, our environment and our positions for any evil that we commit through our idolatry. Some persons even use a declaration of insanity, while others use more ridiculous excuses. The point is, that only a few persons are taking responsiblity for their actions. This, I argue, is the Pilate syndrome.

In the present discussion, Pilate plays a special role as the contradictor of responsibility. In the most damning commentary on his life, he stands in front of the most innocent person this world has ever known, and washes his hands to deny his complicity in the false condemnation. One might ask how in all the world could Pilate act with such deceit in the face of all evident contradictions. Yet, this is the issue behind every irresponsible action namely, that irresponsibility goes its way against the truth. When it wants to have its way it asks the Pilate question, "What is truth?" and without waiting for an answer, pontificates a falsehood as if it is truth.

A simple reading of the Gospels notes the illegal formalities of Pilate's illicit court proceedings. In trying to make the trial acceptable, he by-passed all reasonable ethics. By washing his hands, he thought he could exonerate himself and maybe, the Romans from responsiblity while implicating the Jews. But history has shown that neither he, the Romans, nor the Jews were able to avoid responsibility. In the Psalmists words, "They band together against the righteous and condemned the innocent to death," (Psa 94:21).

The point here is not to argue concerning who is most guilty for the condemnation of Jesus, but to show how our culture of irrresponsiblity has entered into the attitude of "passing the buck." By washing its hands and walking away from its sinful actions it hopes it can make itself acceptable to society. Now as ever, it is argued that taking responsibility when it comes to wrong is not politically safe. To wash the hands like Pilate did, is said to be a most "prudent" way in which one can live respectably. But false respectability which fakes integrity and morality are destructive to a Christian's faith. Let me use a few biblical and literary examples to emphasize the point.

An effort to perfume away responsiblity

In reading Shakespeare's moral mastery pieces one can also find appropriate comments on the political interests and lack of moral responsibility named above. The story of *Macbeth*, for example, shows Lady Macbeth washing her hands and bathing them in perfume to cover her moral indiscretion. She soon finds that perfumes and grand schemes of power pretense could not salvage her conscience. In trying to scheme her anxieties grew. This is why she works so obsessively to hide her transgression. She thinks that by washing her hands a thousand times a day she can cleanse herself. Even in the night when she must rest she walks amidst her sleep and writes out her deeds on scraps of paper, and washes more to put her burdened conscience to rest. Later in the drama Shakespeare brings in a doctor and a gentlewoman who could watch and describe every movement of Lady Macbeth's burdened conscience. When Lady Macbeth rises from her bed to wash her conscience she does so sometimes for a quarter hour. The blood stain of the murdered victims is deep upon her hands

though, and she washes and washes, but still confesses "Yet
here's a spot," and cries out: "Out, damned spot! Out I say!
One; two; why then 'tis time to do't. Hell is murky! Fie, my
lord, fie! a soldier and afraid? What need who knows it, when
none can call our power to account?" (V:i.35)   Falling into
total despair, Lady Macbeth asks the doctor, "What, will these
hands never be clean?" Again she tries to wash, but becomes
exasperated and repeats her confession, "Here's the smell of
the blood still; all the perfumes of Arabia will not sweeten this
little hand." "Oh, oh, oh!" She washes and washes but without
being cleansed. She goes to bed with her madness of guilt.
Her husband is very concerned for her and his own future
when he utters "I have lived long enough, my way of life. Its
fall'n into the sear, the yellow leaf; and which should
accompany old age, as honor, love, obedience, troops of
friends I must not look to have; but, in their stead, curses, not
loud, but deep, mouth-honor, breath which the poor heart
would fain deny, and dare not." (V:iii. 22f). When he sends
for the one whom he hopes can help his conditions, he asks the
doctor:

> Can'st thou not minister to a mind diseas'd.
> Pluck from the memory a rooted sorrow,
> Raze out the written troubles of the brain,
> And with some sweet oblivious antidote
> Cleanse the stuff'd bosom of that perilous stuff
> Which weighs upon the heart? (V:iii. 40)

The doctor replies, "Therein the patient must minister to
himself."   This presses the reality of the murderous
responsibility to the point where neither Lady Macbeth nor
Macbeth could deny it. They had both participated in a terrible
deed and must die for it, either from a stroke or from the
executioners sword.[6]

Confronting responsibility in a puritanical culture

Some four and one half centuries after Shakespeare's *Macbeth,* Nathaniel Hawthorne wrote a critique of the Puritan moral vision in his book the *Scarlet Letter* which attends to the same question of responsibility like *Macbeth.* Hawthorne's novel is not as violent as Shakespeare's but the effort to hide guilt is just as transparent. The story began on a breezy day when a ship docked in the Massachusetts Bay in the town of Boston. On the ship there was a beautiful modest young woman named Hester Prynne. She had traveled to the New World alone, arriving before her slightly deformed scholarly husband of advanced age. As much as she could, she walked about the new community with an air of confidence and quiet dignity. She soon decided to take up residence with the Puritans, some of whom were quick to publicly judge and punish sinful members. All offenders were put to public shame.

Although Hester kept to herself, with the exception of community work, fate had it that she met a young unmarried town minister, Arthur Dimmesdale, who believed in the laws and punishments of the Puritans. He was God-fearing, but had to admit his humanness as he fell into a grave sin. He committed adultery with Hester, but felt that it was better to live with a secret sin than to confess such sin and allow his church to suffer embarrassing consequences. The Puritan people respected him and believed that he was a very "godly" pastor. They would therefore take it very grievously if any scandal fell upon their congregation.

When he became intimately involved in Hesters' life, it resulted in a pregnancy. However, when Hester was found guilty of adultery and the Puritans demanded the name of her accomplice so that he could be hung, she helped to conceal the deed by refusing to name Dimmesdale. She was then led to prison for her silence. On the way to the prison she could see on one side of the prison door a "grass-plot with much overgrown pigweed, while on the other side of the door she saw a rose-bush. The grass-plot was symbolic of her troubles that she would face while the rose-bush represented the good that would come out of the tragic circumstances within her life.

Hester gave birth to a child and named her Pearl. Pearl grew into a beautiful, vigorous and graceful little girl. As she grows she continually worked on Dimmesdale's conscience, impressing upon him to confess publicly. But he agonized over his desire to confess and the consequences that he knew he would face with any confession. As Pearl's presence reminded Dimmesdale of his secret sin, he continued to inflict punishment upon himself. Pearl ever reminded both her parents of their illicit love affair. When, however, the Puritans wanted to take the child away from Hester, she offered to give her life for her child. Once Hester had decided to carry the child full term, she lost respectability in her Puritan society. Pearl was truly Hester's only treasure, her pearl of great price.

One day Hester was brought before the town so that the smug, "goodwives" of the Puritans could have the day of judgment fall upon her. They brought her to the scaffold which was positioned in the center of Boston. That particular day the town was full of people because it was the day of the town meeting. In protest of their condemning attitude Hester held Pearl close to her breast and stood on a scaffold for at least three hours. But she was not hung because two years had passed and there was no proof that her husband was alive. She was thus judged by the Puritans and told that she had to wear the scarlet letter "A," (which stood for adultery), for the rest of her life. The letter was placed upon her breast so that she would be a living sermon against such sins. Many "respectable" individuals sat in judgement observing her punishment, and when she was led to the scaffold the townswomen shouted, "Hang the hussy!" That is, make her an example. When Pearl pointed to the scarlet letter "A" upon Hester's breast she also reminded her mother of her sin.

Though Dimmesdale mingled with the people, he found it most difficult to come forward with his sin. He thus made an appeal to Hester to publicly confess the name of her accomplice, for he wished to deal with his own shame, though he found it hard to come down from his "high place to stand beside her on her pedestal of shame." He really wanted to confess, but he felt that his confession would do more harm than good. Hester later informed him that she did not speak for him for she knew that even though the child's earthly father might not accept her she could look to her Heavenly Father. In Hester's response one could see that while the townspeople had judged based on her outward sin, within her heart she had deeply repented and given over her life to God.

Later in the story Hester's husband, Roger Prynne, found out the perpetrator of the adultery and wished to make a public show of Dimmsdale. To carry out his act of retribution Hester's husband even took on a pseudonym, Roger Chillingworth. He had been well received by the towns-people because they needed a physician. They readily adopted him because he took a special interest in Mr. Dimmesdale, their ailing minister. Physician Chillingworth became a mutual friend of Dimmesdale with the intent of destroying him. Dimmesdale wanted to reject Chillingworth's medical treatment, but it was like a compulsion that Dimmesdale continued to remain under the physician's care. Patient Dimmesdale felt that too much agitation would bring some revelation. When the town's people began to see a look of terror and gloom in Dimmesdale's face and a growing evil in the eyes and face of Chillingworth, they began to wonder if Chillingworth was the Devil himself. Chillingworth even tried some magic on Dimmesdale until he was near death. He thus got more pleasure out of seeing Dimmesdale suffer rather than encouraging him to confess his sin. As Dimmesdale suffered with his pain, his sermons became filled with compassion. The sufferings enabled him to sympathize with the sins and sufferings of his congregation. His congregation, not knowing his guilt, began to see him as a " miracle of holiness." The question for Dimmesdale was whether he should have continued to seek earthly solutions to his problem or whether he should take them to the cross?

When he was near death Dimmesdale went to the scaffold and opened his shirt before the townspeople and upon his chest the people could see the letter"A." Having confessed his sin, a great weight was lifted off his shoulders. Then he fell into Hesters' arms and died. The townspeople were so shocked that a sense of silence fell upon them. They began to ask questions among themselves. "Could it be that their respected minister committed such a sin?" "Could they be sinners as he?" Perhaps the death was to teach a lesson that all of them were sinners. They all were to learn about responsibility.[7]

Infected minds, unnatural deeds: Who else to blame

A popular phrase in common culture is "I didn't do it." We hear it among children and we smile since we know how their tactics for hiding their misdeeds are unsophisticated and they are easily found out. Yet when we have to deal with adults their strategies of denial and disassociation are so complex that not even a lie detector can penetrate the masks. The bestsellers in the movies and on the novel racks show how we humans live with deception and fail to take responsibility. Yes, the public show of innocence, the fear of embarrassment and punishment, the loss of social power, and simple inconvenience are reasons people pass the buck. Until a scandalous media attempts to let out a collected secret of a public figure, there is pretensiveness and personal purity. But there is a haunting reality that ours is a culture with a desensitized conscience.

The agonizing realization of irresponsibility has been the age long issue with Pilate's and Lady Macbeth's handwashing, and Dimmesdale's deception. With Adam and Eve, it was fig leaves. With David it was the murder of Uriah. With Judas it was being present at the supper table though he has betrayed his Lord for thirty pieces of silver. And with some of our modern public characters it is having someone to take the blame on their behalf. It was not laughable when I was told of a certain pastor who had his deacon to accept the blame for the pregnancy of a certain member for him. I have known of another that was a constant terror to the young ladies in his congregation, but he cried in every sermon, calling for purity among the membership. He did all he could to cover his conscience. I have told of these not to attack the ministry, but to make the point that the Pilate syndrome is both in the public political forum and in the context of many churches, as well. It is thus in the latter framework that the writer of Timothy says many persons do everything to scorch their consciences as with a hot iron (1 Tim 4:2). That means, from their reductionist point of view, they give little attention to their individual responsibility and personal guilt. At some stage they might have suffered a bad conscience, but in wanting to save their reputation and enjoy themselves, they dismissed the urging of their consciences and continue their double dealing. If at any time they feel a sense of uneasiness about their artfulness, they wash their hands and move on to their next irresponsible action.

The Christian and responsibility

The point of this discussion has been to dare Christians to confront our culture of irresponsibility and to insist upon a culture of responsibility. In such a case we say that character is more important than reputation, truth is more important than artfulness, and that right is more important than might. A deep concern of mine asks "How can persons in our culture act with truly sensitized consciences?" "How can we let go of our indulgent and pleasure-loving ways?" We see so much evil around us that we sometimes fail to muster the energy to confront it. We participate in it and want to do like Pilate, the Macbeths and Mr Dimmesdale, namely, pretend that we are not a part of it. But if we accept the socio-biological constructions of contemporary behavior, that irresponsibility is natural and therefore normal. We cannot deny our culpability. We speak of the irresponsible as if it has a place in our lives, thus helping to perpetuate the greatest Satanic falsehood of our times. Instead of an attitude of repentance, we seek lowered standards for everything. We remove the boundaries and then blame the circumstances of our lives for the greatest chaos into which we have come.[8]

The question remains, "What will it take to bring our culture to act more responsibly?" What will it take to lead us away from excessive passion and blind rage and the rebelliousness with which we seek to destroy each other. Sooner or later each human being will have to face the question about responsibility, for the challenge of living in a world of irresponsibility means ultimate destruction.[9] Even though humanity seeks to deny it, everyone must confront a life of responsibility. And though each might seek to forget it, yet the answer of history tells us that many human beings have failed to take up their responsibility.

At the heart of our relationship with the divine is the sense of responsibility. Thus we must speak of our moral obligation and of our commitments. To live otherwise is to fail to take note of the authority by which we must live and the norms given to us by God. If the total basis of our belief, our traditions, our values, and our culture is solely humanism, we must call ourselves to repentance. We must insist upon the most fundamental principles by which to live, namely, our duty to God, our boundaries, our choices, our decisions, our individual rights and the rights of others.   Principles of responsibility can be sometimes complex, but each can be simple if we understand that a responsible person will turn to God to help him/her determine moral conduct. I am concerned about the large number of persons, even Christians, who want to dispose of such determination today. It is no wonder that we act with such complicity with the world. Because we often lack the moral conviction and the courage to be committed, we often brace our lives for the worst of errors. I feel a deep sense of pain about the hurt being experienced by many families and the injury they are doing to themselves. I think we need to say something more about responsibility, for there can be no repentance without its deepest understanding. But we are to suspend this present discussion and connect it with other subsidiary ones. Here let it be understood that if we are negligent about our moral obligations we will find a deleterious consequence for our whole society. Thus what will be of interest as we continue future discussions is to know whether if the popular maxims and proverbs we often hear concerning responsibility are still meaningful to us. The following maxims come quickly to mind:

>"Honesty is the best policy."
>"Truth will ultimately win."
>"Love your neighbor as yourself."
>"Do unto others as you would have them do to you."

ENDNOTES

1. Laura Schlessinger (1996), *How could you do that: The Abdication of Character, Courage, and Conscience*, New York:

Harper Collins Publishers, p. 6.

2. H. Richard Niebuhr (1963), *The Responsible Self*, New York: Harper & Row.

3. Ellen White (1917), *Prophets and Kings,* Boise Idaho: Pacific Press Publishing Association, pp 479-490. Quotes could have been taken from many parts of this book which reviews the history of the prophets and the kings of Israel and Judah. In nearly every chapter the moral courage which led to leadership success, over against the weak moral power, the vacillating character, and impaired judgment, which lead to the moral failure of others, has been stated.

4. William Frankena (1966), *Ethics*, (Englewood Cliffs, New Jersey: Prentice Hall, pp. 55-57.

5. Reinhold Niebuhr *(1965), Beyond Tragedy: Essays on the Christian Interpretation of History,* New York: Charles Scribner's Sons. In these essays Niebuhr was focusing on the tragedy of morality in relation to justice and the abdication of Christian prophetic responsibility in critiquing the culture. In the essay in which he spends much time with Pilate he argues that Pilate's chief interest at the trial of Jesus was to make sure that Jesus had no interest in this world, whether Jesus' type of kingship held a threat to the Roman imperium. Then with the assurance that the Kingdom was not of the world, Pilate relaxed and did as he willed. His conscience became easy for he thought he was not to face the divine judgment. However, Niebuhr insists, that before we accept Pilate's complacency, we should inquire further into the nature of the kingdom that is not of this world and note that it is such a kingdom that brings judgment upon the world.

6. William Shakespeare, *Macbeth*, Wilbert J Levy, (1972 ed.) New York: Amisco School Publications.

7. Nathniel Hawthorne, *The Scarlet Letter*, Seymore Gross, et al. eds. (1988) New York: W. W. Norton & Co.

8. Roger Crisp & Christopher Cowton, "Hypocrisy and Moral

Seriousness," *American Philosophical Quarterly*, Vol 4:4, (Oct. 1994), 343-344.

9. Paul Holmer (1988), "Making sense morally," *The Grammar of the Heart: New Essays in Moral Theology and Philosophy,* Richard Bell (ed), New York: Harper & Row, p. 120-123.

CHAPTER TWO

SEXUAL POLITICS AND SEXUAL ETHICS

Sexual politics

Some years ago I read of a young man about whom a grandfather was boasting in public. One day when many people were present, the old man looked around and saw a good-looking woman coming toward him. With a sly look, he stepped beside his grandson and said, "Son, that looks like the woman you had last night." The young man looked up and told his grandpa to go away because he knew that the people who were around him were listening in. But the old man was hurt, and he said, "I said nothing wrong. I simply said, it looked like her. No harm in that, is there?" He was quiet for a few minutes, but continued his observation, "That looks like the lady." The woman's husband was there and overheard, and soon he answered, "Yes, that's the fellow. He was with my wife last night!" When the meeting broke up and everyone went home, the young lady's husband quickly got on his pony and rode over and shot the old man's red burro and killed the grandson's pony. He had only been letting the matter ride until it was made known in public.

A story such as the above may seem crude, but only so because it is from a primitive culture. However, it is modest to what is taking place in he high social circles in our modern metropolitan world. The stories we hear in connection with the politics of power in the metropolitan world, tell that a large percentage of sexual relationships are formed according to the whim and fancies that stem from values of erotic desire and poor moral choice. The stories have passed beyond the bounds of what is morally responsible, but excused as personal issues. Thus the biblical ideal of monogamy is trivialized and families are destroyed. It is my interest therefore to challenge the erotic adventure and narcissistic craving which are being foisted as normal behavior these days. I want to argue from the basis of Christian moral integrity that a life of adultery is superficial and bankrupt. I wish to restate that in our culture we have made a mockery of "the covenant of love" even using pretexts of political correctness.

Love or politics

Who wants to talk about love these days? Love is being spoken about, but only as it affects politics. As my radio scanned the broadcast waves one day, I heard the lines of a song: "Darling I will love you forever, but if we can't get along, tell me, tell me baby, and let us depart." A little later it was the news of the infidel life of some politician. The song did not seem to draw upon the unqualified commitment, firm connectedness, supportive loyalty, and sanctified intimacy, which are at the foundation of the covenant of love and neither did the news. I therefore mused to myself as I said there is no covenant and no love in much of our modern relationships, there is only convenience.

By speaking of a covenant of love I mean to indicate that life is based upon a faithful loyal relationship which God pledges to us in Christ. On a horizontal plane, it is the grace relationship which God gives us to share through the love of Christ. Love that is true is not a natural thing. Though the unredeemed person might love, such love is unstable, self-centered and always corrupted. As Paul shows, the person who lives by the "flesh" lives a life of illusions (Gal 5:19-21). He/she might have good intentions, but the intentions quickly change because the heart is already corrupted (Rom 1, 2, 6, 7).

To abide in love's covenant one must stay within the triangle of divine love. Jesus stated this ideal: "You shall love the Lord your God with all your heart, with all your soul and with all your might, and your neighbor as yourself." (Lk 10:27).

Dealing with the aberrations of love

Only as one understands the above can one focus on the trite ways in which people in our contemporary culture, even in the culture of the Church, have been viewing the covenant of love.   For example, in some sub-cultures of the Church there is support for "shacking up," non-committal, non-monogamous heterosexual behavior, and many other forms of perversions.   I do not make the observation simply to point fingers at sex from a negative perspective, but the intent is to take note of the fact that in a world where much of life is so politically tainted, we need to press for appropriate behavior based on love and faithfulness.

The collector of Proverbs gave much attention to the wisdom of disciplined living and self-control in relation to sexuality. He spoke passionately of the significance of sexual enjoyment, but where he saw sexual irresponsibility he spoke with as much fervor of its destructive power.   In Proverbs 2:16-19; 5:1-14; 6:24-35; 7:1:1-27 he asks his instructees to contemplate the force of [seductors and] seductresses: their coaxing, their sweet, smooth talk, their flattery, their deceit, and their dress, etc.   Then he suggests that their temptation is like the cloak of death.   It is like playing with fire or meeting upon a thief, etc. His point is to suggest that sexual morality is primary for a successful career, a successful marriage and spiritual well being. And who could know better than one who had his career and spiritual life destroyed by his indiscretions.

Lying under oath

A great many persons in our day fail to take with great soberness, the kind of solemn commentary that Solomon makes concerning sexual indiscretions. Even to raise the issue of sexual morality concerning the political leadership in our land is not done so much on the basis of some serious concern for the morals of our culture, as it seems only to make for political gains.[1] If the discussion can win an election or get media ratings, then it is pursued to a most profound depth. However to raise the topic for moral and ethical interests makes one seem Victorian and out of step with contemporary culture. It is of interest that while on the one hand, there is a political call for morality, on the other hand, there is in many churches, a call for compassion even to the point of condoning perversions.

While most married couples see monogamous sexual relationships as respectable at the attitudinal level, at the behavioral level, the norm has become much less rigid. When, for example, political leaders who have called for an impeachment of a president for his sexual indiscretions, while confessing to their own impropriety as normative, one can see an irony. My wife and I were discussing the whole event when she came forth with the most brilliant suggestion I had heard for a while. She said, "Those who take the oath of marriage and practice infidelity are lying under oath in as much as those lying to a Federal Grand Jury. The only difference is that one is breaking the law of the land and the other is breaking the higher law, which is the law of God." A 1990 study which focused on extramarital sex and HIV risks noted that an estimated 26% to 50% of men and 25% to 38% of women reported at least one lifetime occurrence of extramarital sex. The report spoke frequently of "primary" and "secondary" sex partners. It also noted that such kinds of relationships are common across the broad spectrum of marriage though more frequent among younger married couples. It was also common across most racial/ethnic cultures, though more emphasized where a context offered the male greater power of social control. In many cultures extramarital sex is viewed as a sign of male virility. The report also showed that extramarital sex occurred where there was poor sexual communication skills among couples and where persons spent much time idolizing sex. A redeeming aspect of the report states that even among groups where percentages on extramarital sex was high, church-goers tended to report less frequency in the activity.[2]

But an immediate response to the latter might be that wherever there is strong disapproval of extramarital sex respondents were prone to misreport. Another interpretation might be that the biblical ideal of monogamy is acceptable to church-goers not only at the level of theory, but at the level of behavior. If the latter conclusion is correct, we might say "Thanks be to God for roses rare, for skies of blue and sunshine fair. . ." There are redeeming communities in the world, and the Church is the most dynamic one of them.

A point of contradiction to the biblical position is the notion being pushed by evolutionary psychologists that people are not created for monogamous relationships. The discussion focuses on the animal kingdom, and notes that in a majority of species, one male monopolizes a harem of females, while the females of most species are somewhat sexually adventurous. According to Robert Wright, those who are pushing such notions argue that human beings are designed to "fall in love," but not to stay there. It is "natural" for both men and women, at some times, under some circumstances, to commit adultery or "sour a mate," to suddenly find a mate unattractive, irritating, and wholly unreasonable.[3] In effect, such conclusions place moral thinking on a naturalistic basis, then makes the modern world of close neighborhoods, contraceptive technology, erotic movies, sexual explicit billboards, smut magazines, fashion models, and economic inequalities, responsible for all the sexual irresponsibility we see around us.

Fundamentally, it is argued, human beings have the impulse of "wanderlust," so anyone who is permiscuous should still be thought of as normal and responsible. But we know the fallacy of this argument.

Sex and privacy.

Another fallacy of contemporary culture is that sex is a question only for one's own private life. There is privacy when there is a legitimate context, but once it is taken into a public realm where it creates a hazard to the lives of others, then it is no more a private matter. In Scripture we are told: "Therefore a man shall leave his father and his mother and shall cling to his wife and the two of them shall become one flesh" (Gen 2:24). The overall point of the text is that marriage makes for the building of community. I stated at the beginning of this discussion that the axis of successful covenantal community is love and trust. In the context of marriage, a man and woman become wholly committed to each other in love and trust. As they love and trust each other they are given every right to privacy. The wedding ceremony indicates the starting point of this privacy. The fulfillment of conjugal obligations throughout the existence of the marriage becomes the high point of continued commitment to their privacy. Thus when that which certifies the marriage, at its most intimate level, is shared with others, there is a destruction of their privacy and many social dysfunctions occur.

A young lady called me in a very hysterical mood because she heard that her former boyfriend had AIDS. In an effort to calm her I said, I am very sorry for him, however, you should not have to worry so much personally. As soon as I said that she butted in and said: "But you do not understand, while I had been faithful to him he had been sleeping around." I tried to comfort her in every way, but finally could only reassure her of the mercies of God if she would have to face the worse. As I got off the phone, I said to myself, "Yes, there is a lesson here for us." A lesson we can find in the Bible.

The lesson begins with the creation story in which the man and the woman were given to life-long partnership in privacy with each other. While great biblical characters like Abraham (Gen. 16), Jacob (Gen. 30:1-8), Gideon (Judges 8:30), King David (1 Sam. 25:39) and Solomon (1 Kings 9:16) have been named as participants in polygamous and concubinage relationships, nowhere does Scripture seek to place their experience as normative. A superficial reading of Hosea might suggest a contrary scriptural norm when Hosea is told to marry a whore. But a deeper reading will show that the marriage was actually a prophetic action to indict the adulterous practices in Israel and a call for the repentance of the people of God. The charge of God against Israel is explicitly stated by Hosea as "idolatry," "prostitution," "adultery," and "harlotry." The conclusion here is that when people turn away from the covenant of divine love there is no boundary to their practices (see Hosea 7).

In the New Testament the ideal is the same as it is in the Old Testament. The emphasis is upon "one flesh." Jesus responded to the Pharisees' question on divorce with the challenge that "whoever divorces his wife except for unchastity, and marries another commits adultery" (Matt 19:9). There were trivial arguments that allowed a man to put away his wife because he did not find any favor in her, that is because of sterility, insanity, or because he found someone he liked better, or because she burned a meal, or because she was speaking with some man in the street. All of these were challenged by Jesus. As Mark and Luke put it respectively: "Whoever divorces his wife, and marries another commits adultery against her; and if she divorces her husband and marries another she commits adultery," (Mk 10:11,12). "Everyone who divorces his wife and marries another commits adultery, and he who marries a woman divorced from her husband commits adultery," (Lk 16:18). Except in the case of Matthew, the Gospels' prohibition against divorce is absolute. Which is to say that the divine covenanted order from creation was the great point of emphasis in the teachings of Jesus. While several points can be made as to the broader meanings of "one flesh," beyond the sexual connotation, the Gospel writers never seemed to lose sight of the core of its meaning.

Paul later gives the same emphasis as Jesus when he states that "A wife is bound by law to her husband as long as he lives accordingly, she will be called an adulteress if she lives with another man while her husband is alive. . . But if her husband dies, she is free from the law, and if she marries another man, she is not an adulteress" (Rom 7:2,3). Further, the husband should give his wife her conjugal rights, and likewise the wife to her husband. For the wife does not have authority over her own body, but the husband does; likewise the husband does not have authority over his own body, but the wife does (1 Cor 7:3,4).

At the heart of both statements stands the unshared sexual obligation which each partner in the marital relationship must have for the other. And the counsel here, as elsewhere, speaks of the nature of human sexuality established in the creation. To the Romans (Rom 1), like the Corinthians (1 Cor 5-7), and to every Christian, Paul uplifts the dignity of monogamous sex over against "casual", "flirtatious", and "permiscuous" sex. Any casual form of sexual relationship, that is such sexual relationship as stands outside of the divine covenant, is seen in the Bible as an action of immorality (or what is referenced as adultery and fornication) (*porneia*). In 1 Cor. 7 where Paul gives a response to the Corinthian Christians on marriage and sexual practices, there is the note that, "...because of cases of sexual immorality (*porneias*) each man should have his *own* (*eautou*) wife and each wife should have her *own* (*idion*) husband." (1 Cor 7:2). There are many arguments as to the meaning of the word "immorality" (*porneia*), such as whether it has to do with adultery (generally thought of as extra-marital sex), or whether it deals with fornication (generally thought of as pre-marital sex) or whether it has to do with incest. No one seems to be certain of its meaning except to say that the word is used interchangeably and points to immoral sexual acts. Whatever its specific meaning, Paul makes clear that all immoral acts (*porneias*) are considered unnatural by God and are not to be a part of Christian life (see 1 Cor 5-7).

Some biblical exegetes , have argued that Paul compromises the reason for marriage when he notes that "to avoid immorality let every person have their own spouse" (1 Cor 7:1). They would like Paul to answer if the basis of marriage is the avoidance of immorality? Is the central purpose of marriage sex? Careful reading of the passage would suggest that Paul did not intend to depreciate the beauty of the marital state. But from the specific situation of Corinth and from the specific conditions of all cultures of immorality, Paul makes a practical point "let every person have his/her *own* spouse." Contemporary conditions are showing us the full consequences of unchastity. Sexually Transmitted Diseases (STDs), high rates of divorce and separation, one parent (single parent) families, high rates of abortion, violence of all sorts, only partly describe the tragic conditions of an irresponsible culture.

The greatest emphasis of Paul is the impact of immorality on one's personal and spiritual life:

> The body is meant not for fornication but for the Lord, and the Lord for the body...Do you not know that your bodies are members of Christ? Should I therefore take the members of Christ and make them members of a prostitute? Never! Do you not know that whoever is united to a prostitute becomes one body with her? For it is said, "The two shall

be one flesh." But anyone united to the Lord becomes one spirit with him. Shun fornication! Every sin that a person commits is outside the body; but the fornicator sins against the body itself. Or do you not know that your body is a temple of the Holy Spirit within you, which you have from God, and that you are not your own? For you were bought with a price; therefore glorify God in your body (1 Cor 6:13-20).

Sex and the Body

By using the foregoing text one can attend to three critical issues which Paul like Christ sought to emphasize. One has to do with the impact of sexual immorality on the body, another with sexual immorality on the mind and the other is the impact of sex on the spirit. Paul like Christ understood these issues profoundly and sought to correct the idolatrous ways in which the body, mind and spirit were being used. Noting his insights from Romans 1 and other passages, we see how much Paul was aware of a culture that exploited the body for sexual gratification. He knew that the Greeks were preeminent for the practice of homosexuality while the Romans seemed to specialize in heterosexual promiscuity. For a dominant part of Greek and Roman cultures, anything in which the body found satisfaction was acceptable.

Contemporary culture combines the Greeks' and Romans' emphasis on the body, but has even surpassed those cultures in its idolatry. As many social scientist have found, much economic benefit is gained from "body politics." Some say, "sex and politics make good theater." Others say, "body language makes good money." Thus we see the body is worshiped everywhere.

Paul Schiller, who has done an extensive analysis of the body, says that the image of the human body forms a picture in our minds. Any stimulated part of the body leaves a special impression on the sensory cortex. We must therefore be conscious of the stimuli that we allow to enter our bodies for they affect our physical, psychological, moral and spiritual selves.[5] If all Schiller says is also true, then one needs to be careful how one shares oneself in sexual relationships with others for one always leaves pieces of one's consciousness with others. In one of Chaplain Barry Black's sermons he tells of a young man who came to him in despair. The young man stated that he could not explain how he had AIDS since he was not a run around. But he muttered under his breath that he only had sex once with a young lady he did not know. The chaplain muttered back, "Well, likely you had sex with all of the persons she had sex with." The point being made is that sex leaves memories and creates flashbacks which, if not pleasant, causes personal destruction. And since the sexual act unites (Gk. *kollao*) the bodies of two beings into one (body), one has to be most conscious about how one unites with another.

Sex and the mind

Even though he did not make particular reference in the above text, yet in many places Paul gives emphasis to the impact of false pleasures on the mind. In Romans 8:6 he notes that "To set the mind on the flesh is death, while to set the mind on the Spirit is life and peace." In Romans 1 he speaks of those who practiced sexual aberrations as those with "debased minds." The mind as we understand it is the most intimate (private) part of one's being. When Jesus spoke of adultery as a sin of the "heart" he was using the understanding of the culture in which he lived that the heart was the most intimate part on one's being. However, if he were living in our time he might have said that adultery is a sin of the mind. The impact of this point is to say that infidelity is not so much a sexual act as it is the sharing of one's most intimate being with one to whom one is not covenanted. Most of the cases of infidelity which are reported by the media are not cases of sex, but the sharing of intimacies with other(s) than one's partner to the extent that disruptions are caused in the covenanted relationship. However, one understands the mind whether as total consciousness or as the extension of the body, it is clear that when one is involved in infidelity the mind is carried away.

Sex and the spirit

A further point touched upon by Paul in regards to sex and the body is that the body is the temple of God. To desecrate the body is to deface the *temple* (the inner sanctum) (*hieron*) of God. When the body is defaced devils take it over. It is therefore of importance that believers protect their spiritual territory. Thus when believers are joined to Christ they come into a unity of mind, soul, and spirit that is unique (1 Cor 2:16). They cannot practice anymore acts that are against Christ. Any act that is against the body insults Christ. Our bodies belong to God by creation and for the redeemed it belongs to God by redemption. "You are bought with a price" (1 Cor 6:20). The spiritual, psychological and mental aspects of our being are therefore to be protected.

Another way of stating the above is to say that sexual sins start from within. Since sexual activity permits profound self-disclosure[6] when one is involved in illicit sex one is bound to disclose a lot about one's lustful spirit. A fact that has always interested me in the confession of drug traffickers is that they try to avoid sexual contact with a person they love as much as they can since they are afraid that they will disclose something. They have affirmed correctly that in the sexual act, one is breaking open his/her inner being. This is why anyone who looks at a person with a lustful eye, has already committed adultery in his/her heart. (Matt 5:28). And since human sexuality reflects at its highest, the creative and transformative power of God, and at its lowest, the most destructive force in the world, every thing should be done to use sex in a positive direction. By this I mean that one needs to treat it with respect, focus on the effectiveness of its relational power and use it with responsibility. These three ideas demand further development.

Sex and respect for others

According to the *Webster New International Dictionary*, respect has to do with, among others things, "consideration" of others, "regard" and "esteem" of self and others. It also means "personal honor." When such is connected to the second great commandment, "You shall love your neighbor as yourself" (Matt 19:18; 22:39; Lev 19:18) it will make a great difference for how one treats the other in a sexual relationship. In reality, respect begins with the self before it can be passed on to others. And the self has to be valued or esteemed and appreciated. Self-appreciation, self-regard, self-realization, and self-sacrifice, are common terms we hear every day and they are opposite of self-deception, self-devaluation, self-hatred, self-deprecation and self-destruction. For one to esteem oneself one has to see the self as created in the image of God (a point which we have emphasized throughout our discussion). To esteem others one must also think of them as part of the *imago dei*. A negative form of the great commandment reads, "What is hateful to thee do not do to thy neighbor. That is the whole law. All else is commentary upon it."[7] The point is that in a relationship where respect rules, all persons in the relationship will see to the dignity of the other. The body and all the rest of the being will be seen as the place of the divine sanctuary, in which case, all forms of violence will be avoided.

Sex and relationship building

An extension of the above point is to note what part sex plays in relationship building for sex has creative and unitive power. Those who get caught up in superfluous forms of sexual relations have at some point, taken their relationships for granted. They emphasize technique more than relationship and lose their relationship.

At the heart of sexual relationship is trust and love. Trust includes what we ordinarily think of as faith and faithfulness, commitment and loyalty, integrity and purity. To say this another way, we can note that it is faith, not emotion, that makes a sexual relationship grow. In marriage, faith in husband and wife is a practical and dynamic force. Under the most difficult circumstance faith still affirms the best because it is tough, hard-headed, and determined for commitment. From faith we get the term fidelity. Infidelity is therefore the tragic act of breaking the strongest link in the chain of a relationship. Roberta Israeloff says that infidelity in the family is like a "wrecking ball" that leaves chaos in its wake. Those who get hurt feel betrayed and filled with rage. Actions of infidelity also extend hurt upon children, friends, churches and other communities, as well. Whole communities of persons are often drawn into the unfaithfulness of two people.[8] I have known of one occasion when a husband was practicing infidelity and figured that his wife was about to find out and would share the burden with her close female friend. As the husband thought so it happened. But to assure himself, the husband had tapped his own phone to sneak in on any conversation his wife would share with her friend. The day he called his wife's friend and threatened her to stay out of his life, she was shocked. She knew she was drawn into a situation she had least suspected. But it was too late. She found that what she had heard was true. Most adulterers work through stages of lying, denying, minimizing and blaming so that their sinful actions seem excusable. The greatest deception of an adulterer is the denial of violence that is brought into a family.

The other fundamental aspect of relationship building for sexual life is love. Love is not separate from faith and fidelity, but is central to both. In a faithful sexual relationship love rules. What many persons call love is only the erotic sensual aspect of sexual relation. In many cultures there is the euphemism that people are "making love." But the erotic is only a minor aspect of love. One needs not say the erotic is not an aspect of love for in biblical realism it is spoken of as a normative aspect of sexual relation.[9] Scripture also interconnects the erotic or romantic with affection, loyalty, admiration, kindness, mercy, sacrifice and choice. Biblical love is pure and stands against any secular understanding that suggests that erotic love puts an end to all reflection and sets all senses in a frenzy in which no choice, nor will is left. The person who is gripped by the tyrannical omnipotence of erotic love will find him/herself mastered by it. In the Greek culture the god *Eros* led a person to sensual intoxication. It is against this culture that the Bible stands and uses the word *agape* as the definition of love in which understanding love places reason, concern, compassion, kindness, sacrifice, freedom and respect as the boundry of relationships.

As history has shown, many family tensions between husbands and wives are built on lust (eros), not love (agape). Where agapic love is practiced, one partner seeks to serve the true joy of the other partner. Where lust is practiced, self is served. The attitude of a rapist for example, is to insult his/her victim, not merely for sexual satisfaction, but to demean and depreciate him/her. In any sexual relationship where lust is practiced there is evidence of the fantasies of the rapist. The manipulation, control and violence create the tide of terror that leads to the shadow of death. Novelists have framed the reality under such titles as "Death in the bed of love," etc. But what makes for the great novels is the historical notes on the growing problem of a history of irresponsibility.

Sex and Responsibility

I speak of responsibility on the question of a dignified sexual relationship, for there is need to challenge the irresponsibility of a licentious culture. In the stewardship of life we speak of responsibility as the constructive power that builds community. Thus when one fails to emphasize responsibility in the sexual aspect of life, one allows for tragic social destruction, even upon the innocent. A person who is sexually responsible is not necessarily one who uses prophylactics (condoms or other forms of protection), or one who has an abortion for purpose of contraception while at the same time having an adulterous, fornicating, or otherwise immoral life. The responsible person is one who understands the relation of responsibility to the divine order. In divine the order, sex requires chastity, virginity, and monogamy. Such an order also stands against the myths that say sexual variety, and adventurous, compulsive sexual behavior, including premarital and extramarital sexual relationships, are acceptable norms of life. In the positive sense responsibility calls for personal discipline for the sake of the most profound relationship of intimacy between two persons. It calls for accepting the restrictions of monogamy because it ensures the holistic satisfaction of partners. It also seeks to understand the sexual socialization process; how one approaches today's atmosphere of freedom and equality, the way in which trust is built between partners, and how affections and confidences are shared, etc. In the responsible sexual relationship one recognizes that multiple relationships depend on deceit, evasiveness and superficiality. If one has ever been caught off guard like David, the responsible person will turn back to pray, "Keep back you servant also from the insolent; do not let them have dominion over me. Then I shall be blameless and be innocent of the great transgression." (Psa 19:13).

From the perspective of sexual responsibility one can manifest grace, care, tenderness, protection for a lover and regulate sex in a way that is enriching rather than impoverishing, self giving rather than selfish, respectful rather than dominating. Because a sexual relationship is part of other contingent relationships, responsibility demands that all who participate in such actions calculate with care all contingent relations. So while in a calculated or unintended immoral relationship one or two people might be "enjoying" themselves, there are potential hurts for others who might be related to their relationship. In the experience of love and commitment sex is a rich, strong, vigorous expression of human nature. The Christ-like person can therefore stand by the values that bring its greatest fulfillment. He/she can make decisions that will keep the health and enjoyment in it.

ENDNOTES

1. The News media reports during many political campaigns have borne out the hypocrisy of a moral culture which seems to trivialize sexual impropriety in some cases while in others indict it.
2. Kyang-Hee Choi, "Extramarital Sex and HIV Risk: Behavior Among U.S. Adults: Results from the National Aids Behavioral Survey," *American Journal of Public Health* (Dec 1994) 2003-2007.
3. Robert Wright, "Hearts," *Time*, (August 15, 1994) 45-53.
5. Paul Schilder, "Image and appearance," *The Self in Social Interaction,* (eds, Chad Gordon and Kenneth Gergen), New York: John Urley & Sons Inc., 107-136.
6. Leon Morris, Gen. ed. (1987) , *I Corinthians*: *Tyndale New Testament Commentaries,* Grand Rapids, MI: WM. B.

Eerdmans, 97.

7. See, Charles Briggs (Gen. ed), *The Gospel According to St Matthew, ICC*, New York: Charles Scribness, (1907), where it is noted that the negative form of the Love commandment is ascribed to the school of Hillel (Matt 22:39).

8. Roberta Israeloff, "Surviving Infidelity," *Parents* (June, 1996) 111-112.

9. G. A. Turner, "Love," *The International Standard Bible Encyclopedia,* Vol 3 (Gen ed). G Bromiley, (1986), Grand Rapids, Mi.: Wm. B. Eerdmans.

10. cf. Ezekiel 1: 6; 6:36; 23:57; Hosea 3:1 and Songs of Solomon.

CHAPTER THREE

THE ATTACK UPON THE INNOCENT

Sex abuse as a distressing social problem

I was standing at the door of the Church saying good-bye to the worshipers when she came towards me with her shy looks and an evident angry feelings. She was the little girl that I had left in a certain church I had pastored nearly two years before. As she shook my hand she whispered, "Pastor, can I speak with you in your office for a brief moment?" I told her I would be there soon after the greetings and good-byes were over. As I went to my office she began to tell a sad story. "The reason I am here is that I was forced to leave home to find refuge in a Catholic Hostel because my father had been abusing me for many weeks. When I tried to report it to my mother he threatened to kill her and me. I don't want to cause any problems for my mother, so I took the train and came here."

You don't need to be a pastor or a social worker to say this sounds familiar. The stories can be multiplied. Interesting estimates of the contemporary national situation say that incest occurs in 1 in 6 families in the United States. One estimate says that about 100,000 cases occur each year.[1] Another says that some 3000 cases of child sex abuse are reported yearly in New York City and about half that number in the metropolitan Washington, D.C. area.[2] About a decade ago, the National Center on Child Abuse and Neglect estimated that as many as 500,000 children were sexually abused.[3] Other researchers estimate that 250,000 children are sexually molested by relatives every year and that 2 million families are involved in sexual abuse. In all the samples that I have read from Finkelhour, Baker and Duncan, Ellerstein and Canavan, et al, I have found rates running from six to twenty-three percent. Whether these random estimates are to be taken with seriousness is often a question. However, they are serious enough to make us aware that we are confronting a problem which is profoundly destructive in hundreds of personal lives and their families. Many newspapers across the United States are showing how the tragedy is extending with a number of Day Care Centers getting caught up in incest scandals. A case of a few years ago, showed that some forty-five children in one Day Care Center were involved in sex abuse, though not incest.

Compared to other classes of crimes, sex crimes of all types are generally under reported. There is still a strong public attitude of disapproval toward the victim of a sex crime, as if such a thing doesn't happen to decent people. In adult rape cases, for example, the victim is often badly treated by the police, courts, and lawyers. Sexual abuse of children often involves trusting family members like fathers, stepfathers and siblings. Sometimes preference is given to the protection of the family as a unit rather than to the individual child. Thus one parent may fail to report the sexual abuse of a child. This is even more critical in the case of mothers who fear that if their husband is encarcerated, the financial security of the family will be jeprodized. Other cases are not reported because the child or adult does not know whom to trust or whom to turn for help, seeing that many times they are not believed.

Solid statistics on sexual abuse come from reported cases. Beyond that, one can only guess at how many unreported cases there are. The major sources of reported cases are police and court records, hospitals, mental health clinics, and child abuse hot lines. Some of these sources deal largely with criminal acts and do not cover abuse that may not be immediately considered criminal in nature. There is further bias due to the fact that the legal system and the public health network may be more likely to deal with poor people rather than the middle and upper class offenders.

In spite of these limitations on data, it is informative to look at representative figures. Thus it is noted that one girl in every four in the United States will be sexually abused in some way before she reaches the age of 18. It is also noticeable that if one uses a race/ethnic analysis, then one in four white middle-class females, have had an unwanted preadolescent sex experience of some sort with an adult male.[4] Various types of such abuse are cited below:

> 1. The intra-familial where the abuse occurs with siblings, mother-child, father-child, grandfather-grandchild, and step-father-child.
> 2. The extra-familial where the abuse occurs mostly outside the home with friends and acquaintances who act as surrogates.
> 3. The public criminal type in which pedophiles organize their abusiveness by gaining the confidence of children.

Whatever the type of the abuse, the point here is to declare them as being of an evil character. And that while attention needs to be paid to pedophiles, closer attention needs to be paid to families, for that is where most of the worst criminal acts have started.

Incestuous Families

A word needs to be said of incestuous families because it is believed that the kind of family most likely to suffer incest are dysfunctional types. However, such assumption misses the point that even "well to do" families show evidence of incest. In fact, there are two types of incestuous families:

a. The classic, usually middle upper class which is
seldom known to the courts or the social worker.
b. The multiple problem type which occurs mostly
in the chaotic family where sex abuse is only one of
the many pathologies.

The case I mentioned at the opening point of the
discussion was not from a family identified as dysfunctional.
The mother and father both held church offices. Both were
well respected among their community members. Even the
young lady had looked happy six months before when I had
seen her. That was why I felt quite shocked and sad when she
rehearsed her story to me. But I quickly came to believe her
story. What she did was quite dramatic for any seventeen year
old. I had also previously read narratives of some movie stars,
ministers and teachers who had come to be the perpetrators of
the "hidden sin" thus her story was even more believable.

The hidden sin - seducing the innocent

Many social scientists have called sex abuse among
children the "hidden crisis."[5]   Others have called it "hidden
victims" to emphasize the fact that it is the most *denied,
concealed, distressing* and *controversial* subject to be
discussed.[6] The title of Wilson Keys (1981) book, *Seduction
of the Innocent,* makes the point how subtleties are used to
abuse the innocent. Victims of such abuse are often sworn to
silence and secrecy, so that the perpetrators can carry forward
their actions without discovery. From the many heart
wrenching cases to which I have listened, the most common
denominator is the "unhealthy silence." The fact of silence was
what struck me most deeply when I read a newspaper headline
upon disembarking from an airplane in Jamaica W.I. sometime
ago. Not only was the victim sworn to secrecy, but the
victim's mother became aware of the crime and was sworn to

silence because she believed that if she challenged her husband or reported the crime he would be sent to jail. The tragedy of the story got worse for when the case was made known and taken to court, the judge accepted an apology from the perpetrator with the comment that he feared to send him to jail since he was the only bread winner in the family. The choice of the judge might seem rational if one assumes that jail is not an effective punishment for criminals. However, the decision trivialized the case since the victim remained a victim. She was placed with some other relatives who were to care for her. However, the relative soon began to blame her for allowing her step-father to be disgraced. The shame, the blame, the violence perpetrated against any victim of incest is reason for powerlessness.

The powerful over the powerless

As one thinks of incest one can only see it as the powerful seeking to destroy the powerless. Two dominating things about power and control in an incestuous situation are that (1) it uses the trust of the weaker to destroy and (2) it seeks to make the weaker a co-dependent. Children are naturally dependent on adults. It is therefore not difficult to manipulate them, and play mind-games with them until they are brought into a position where they will be totally vulnerable. The perpetrator of incest can therefore effect full self gratification on all levels.

Perpetrators of sex abuse are generally over the age of 18. They are thus generally significantly older than their victims, and are in a position of power to control the vulnerable. Fathers or mothers, baby sitters, pastors or priests, teachers, and other surrogates who encourage such abuse are criminals of a special kind. The abuse involves violence and coercion since the perpetrator must hold the victim to ransom. While rapists use guns, knives, and other dangerous weapons to make a demand, creating a crisis of life or death, the child sex abuser uses deceptions through kissing, handling, stroking, caressing, oral genital contact or any other form of physical exploitation that lead a victim to vulnerability. There are two things to watch in this direction: (1) There might be an apparent voluntary agreement between victim and perpetrator. In this context the perpetrator leads the victim through a series of confused relationships until the victim seems to agree with the action. (2) There might also be no apparent agreement, though the victim is receiving some degree of pleasure or is threatened to secrecy by the stronger person whose sexual needs are being satisfied by the non-voluntary submission of the weak.

What is the Christian's responsibility in regards to incest?

Wherever child sex abuse may be occurring, it is crucial that Christians take the lead in helping to ameliorate the situation. First, the Christian needs to have accurate information on how to confront the problem and recommend it for treatment. There is also a need to know the characteristics which identify the sexually abused person and the context of the abuse. Such emotions as irritability, depression, anxiety and introversion are to be addressed otherwise the Church will be complicitous in the abuse. Dr. Joseph Peters quoted in a book called *The Best Kept Secret: Sexual Abuse of Children* (1980), has said that one should watch for signals such as loss of appetite, nightmare, bedwetting, clinging to mother, resistance to going to school or playing with friends, severe depression, psychosis, suicidal and homicidal ideation and attempts.[7] When the problem is identified everything possible should be done to help the victim. Some forms of help which might be rendered include:

1. Teaching how to report the crime to the

appropriate authorities.
2. Providing professional help to the victim of the crime.
3. Providing guidance to the family of the victim.
4. Helping to deal with probationary action strategy for the family of the victim.
5. Provide safe environment for victim(s) and their families.
6. Help provide and access therapy for the victim.
7. Provide education to the community in which the abuse occurred or might occur.

If the Church does not engage in practical strategies to deal with child sex abuse it will allow for unhealthy practices to destroy the fabric of our society. While the practical strategies named above are not named in Scripture, Scripture is not the less emphatic about the way in which such kinds of abuse is to be treated.

Sex abuse and church discipline

It is instructive how the Apostle Paul spoke to the Church at Corinth concerning a case of incest. He spoke of a kind of incestuous relationship that is uncommon in our culture, yet he identified points that are powerful for application anywhere. The case consists of a man having sexual relations with his step-mother and the toleration of the church.

It is actually reported that there is sexual immorality among you, and of a kind that is found not even among pagans; for a man is living with his father's wife. And you are arrogant. Should you not have mourned that the sexually immoral should have been removed from among you? For though absent in the body, I am present in the spirit; and as if present I have pronounced judgment in the name of the Lord Jesus on the man who has done such a thing. When you are assembled, and my spirit is present with the power of our Lord Jesus, you are to hand this man over to Satan for the destruction of the flesh, so that his spirit may be saved in the day of the Lord. Your boasting is not a good thing. Do you not know that a little yeast leavens the whole lump of dough? Clean out the old yeast so that you may be a new batch, as you really are unleavened. For our paschal lamb Christ has been sacrificed. Therefore let us celebrate the festival, not with the old yeast of malice and evil, but with the unleavened bread of sincerity. (1 Cor 5:1-8).

Paul does not hide the fact that he is shocked that the Church is suffering disrepute. He spoke frankly about punishment for the perpetrator of the crime. We can gain some principles from the challenge he sets forth, namely:

1. That an evil as serious as incest cannot be minimized by the Church (or Christian family).
2. That the attitude of pride added to the practice of incest makes its perpetrator more demonic. The same is to be said for any community which tolerates it, for it is the pride that leads to the minimalization of sin.
3. That Christian freedom falsely appropriated will lead to the grossest of evil in a persons life.
4. That sins such as incest, when found in a community should lead the community to bereavement (*epanthesate*) (just as if a member had died) because it means the death of the family and the community.
5. That the offender (perpetrator) of the abuse is to

be judged by the community.

6. That the offender is to be removed (excommunicated) from the community.

7. That the offender is to be punished by the community.

8. The form of punishment involved is handing over the perpetrator to Satan so that the devil might have his way of destruction, unless the offender is transformed and wishes for restoration.

9. That the sin of incest, though grievous, does not constitute the unpardonable sin, so that if the offender repents he will be saved in the day of Christ's appearing.

10. That when the offense of abuse is summarily treated there will be the possibility for community unity and regard for the Church.[7]

How the church can protect the innocent

The fact that the case cited above has to do with adults instead of parent/child etc, does not make it any more acceptable in the community. From the Pauline perspective, incest is incest, immorality (*porneia*) is immorality (*porneia*). The Church and family in which incestuous practices are found must follow the path suggested by Paul. If there is ever temptation to participate in any cover up of incest, such must be resisted. There must be the greatest appreciation of the innocent whose lives are dependent on the adult.

In the teaching of Jesus we find a commentary on the tragedy of destroying the innocent. It reads:

If any of you put a stumbling block before one of these little ones who believe in me, it would be better for you if a great millstone were fastened around your neck and you were drowned in the depths of the sea. Woe to the world because of stumbling blocks. Occasions for stumbling are bound to come, but woe to the one by whom the stumbling block comes! (Matt 18:6-7).

In its context, the text carries a double meaning of how one treats a disciple (or an initiate, who was seen as a childlike person) or a literal child. Also, there is no contradiction that the latter is being emphasized by Jesus for He had a profound interest in the attitude displayed toward them. In His total work He was very concerned about their welfare. He always hated to see them hurt. He spoke of the burden of the one who would invite the child into sin. He spoke of anyone who sought to violate the body of the innocent, to manipulate, control and overpower them and then pretend innocence. He understood that such an attack left the child with perpetual wounds and scars, and feelings of depersonalization. He argued that to sin against them must be looked upon with a particular disgust by God.

Anyone who pushes another to participate in sin helps to perpetuate sin. When sin is taught to the innocent a train is set in motion. Thus "the sins of the father is passed on the to the third and fourth generation." Persons who have been abused become abusers, persons who have been oppressed become oppressors; some suffer eating disorders, some become co-dependents, and others sexual deviants. The conditions of helplessness, hopelessness and alienation are multiple and severe. This should therefore give a person reason to pause and consider the burden of starting an evil train in society. Although one can see that thousands are getting away from being caught today, one can say with Isaiah, that anyone who acquits the guilty of their bribe and deprive the innocent of their rights will be judged by God. (See Isa 5:23). Until the final act of divine judgment, one of the major tasks of all God-fearing persons is to protect the innocent, that is to find ways to act with justice and righteousness to deliver them from the hand of oppressors who rob them of their lives (Jerm 22:3).

ENDNOTES

1. C. A. Plummer, (1984) "Preventing sexual abuse activities and strategies for those working with children and adolescents," *Sexual Abuse Fact Sheet*, Homes Beach, Florida, Learning Publishers.   Ellen Bass and Laura Davis, (1988), The Courage to Heal: A Guide for Women Survivors of Child Sexual Abuse, New York: Harper and Row.
2. J. Borken & L. Frank, Sexual Abuse Prevention for Preschoolers: A Pilot Program, Child Welfare League of America, 65 (1) 73-77.
3. D. Sefarino, (1979) *Special Report*: An estimate of nation wide incidence of sexual offenses against children, Child Welfare (58) 127-133. cf. Richard Lacayo, "Whose Child is This," *Time*, (January, 19, 1987), 56-58.
4. cf Jane F Gilgun, "We Shared Something Special: The Moral Discourse of Incest Perpetrators," *Journal of Marriage and Family*, 57 (May 1995) 265-281
5. Carol Poston and Karen Lison, (1989) *Reclaiming Our Lives: Hope For Adult Survivors of Incest*, Boston: Little Brown and Company. Milton J. Senn, Speaking out for America's Children, New Haven: Yale University Press, 1977.
6. C. Adams & J. Fay, (1981), *No More Secrets. Protecting Your Child From Sexual Assault*. San Luis Obispo, Calif.: Impact Publishers.
7. Leon Morris (1990) *Tyndale New Testament Commentaries: 1 Corinthians*, Grand Rapids, Mich.: William B. Eerdmans Publishing Company. cf. William Barclay, (1975) The *Letters to the Corinthians*, Philadelphia Penn.: The Westminster Press.

CHAPTER FOUR

RAPE AND RESPONSIBILITY

The case is rape

She had gone on a vacation to see her mother at a beautiful homestead on the tiny tropical island she had left some thirty years before. She had been back on the island a number of times, but there was to be no visit so memorable as this one. She had gotten to the homestead the evening before with her younger sister. They slept the night and the next morning decided to visit friends in other parts of the island. Upon returning home, they stopped to see their great grandmother who was more than one hundred years old. They had a great time with her and laughed heartily as they drove away in their rented car. As soon as they came to the last corner before they could see the house on the homestead, they noticed something strange - the road was blocked. They stopped to see what was the problem and noticed two men coming out of the nearby bushes. The men quickly came up to them, one brandishing a giant knife which he placed at the throat of the older sister. The other man went to the other side of the car and asked the younger sister to hand over all the money they were carrying. Having received the money which they thought not enough, the men demanded more and threatened to rape the women.

The older sister, sensing the gravity of the moment, and felt that there was no way out but rape or death, said to the men, "If you must rape anyone take me, my children are grown, she [that is my younger sister] has younger children and they will need her so please let her go." In response to her plea, the men took the older sister from the car, and told the younger sister to run. Then they pushed the older sister over a wall and ravished her. They did not kill her but left her terribly injured. In order for them to stop ravishing her she faked a heart attack. But other physical conditions were real; her knees were cut all over; she felt sick to her stomach; her head was spinning and she could barely move. When the ordeal was over and the men ran away, she found that she was still alive and was able to get up and walk to the house. There she found her sister trembling. The raped sister she felt "like dirt." She also full of rage. She felt as though she wanted to kill someone.

After saying a few words to her sister, she was able to collect herself enough to get to the bathroom and wash until she felt a little of the dirt being washed away. The dirt she felt was not physical really, it was deep. The water could not remove it that night. She completed the washing however, and got dressed for bed because she knew she had to sleep or die. She prayed as much as she could, asking God to help her get some sleep so she could blank out everything. She could hardly believe when she got up the next morning that she had slept all through the night.

As soon as she awoke, the intense rage to castrate and kill the rapists returned. At the same time she was getting quite nervous that such horrific thoughts were controlling her. She had grown up in a Christian family and was a person of profound faith. She could not accept the fact that she could even think such thoughts. But it was as if she couldn't stop the feelings now. She left the house and walked to the nearest store and began to tell the story of how two young men robbed her and her sister "last night". She did not really want to talk about the rape, so she only told the store owner that the men really hurt her badly.

Somehow when the man with the knife took her to the

front of the car that the night, she had seen his face. So when the store owner asked her if she could identify the men she responded that yes she thought she could. "In fact," she said, " I think I could tell you right now a few things about him." She told him those things and before she could finish the store owner said "I think I know who they are". He left his store with her, took her back to her home and told her to go visit the doctor. While she went to the doctor he went to the police station and reported the matter. The police sent out an investigation team and before the end of the day, the two criminals were apprehended. In the course of the next week the case was tried. The fellows were charged with aggravated assault and received a two year sentence in jail. It was one of the quickest cases ever tried on the island.

Of course, the court scene was one of the easiest parts of the trial the sister faced. At the end of the week when the raped sister was supposed to preach in a church on the island, she began to wrestle with herself whether she was clean enough. She asked God for strength and felt that she was given the strength to preach. But her real ordeal came when she returned to the United States. As soon as she disembarked she began to feel physically drained, a sense of worthlessness, loneliness, depression, and a cynicalness about every man with whom she came in contact. She could trust no one. She was afraid to venture from her home at night. She also began to have flashbacks and nightmares. She was yelling and screaming almost every night. As her feelings became more intense, she felt she needed help from someone, so she went to see her pastor. The pastor knew her to be a very active church member and a strong Christian. When she told him her story he said to her, "Sister you are strong enough, you should try and handle it." He did not visit her or pray with her. The pastor's attitude heightened her anger and feelings of isolation. In a few days she began to have migraine headaches and chest pains and soon suffered a heart attack.

While she was laying in a hospital bed she was praying and asking God why and how could all this happen. But it seemed that for some three months God was silent. The more she prayed, the more she sensed the stillness of the nights and the loudness of the days. Neither in the stillness nor in the loudness could she hear a word from God. This led her to think that she was dying. Added to all the physical and psychological stresses, her business fell apart and she was on the brink of declaring bankruptcy. It really took her years of struggling before she began to heal and have energy enough to rebuild her business.

When I asked about the source of her healing she told me several things. One was the man who became her husband. The very store owner who helped her identify the criminals to the police, became a trusted friend and later her husband. He married her with the knowledge that she was having many nightmares and other symptoms that went along with the aftermath of rape. When she had the nightmares and flashbacks and became hostile toward him, he would take the hostility and encourage her to calm down. He cared for her until she could accept herself again.

A second part to her healing was the friends who called and gave her needed support. At times when she became angry and would wish them to stay away, they still called and assured her that there is a God who was hearing her prayers and someday would bring her healing.

The third and most important aid to her healing was when she began to "take some kind of responsibility in dealing with the rape." Taking responsibility did not mean blaming herself for the rape or blaming her sister for not hanging around with her. It meant finding a way to forgive the men. The forgiveness really began in the court room when she saw the men and could look them in the eyes. Instead of anger she began to feel a profound sadness for them. But it was in the hospital in the United States that she felt that she would have to forgive them and see them as children of God. Instead of praying for their death, she began to pray that somehow God might save them. She also began to feel that not every man was a rapist. In fact, it was not long until she began to correspond with the man who had helped her the morning after the rape and subsequently became his wife.

Her healing continued when she began to share her experience with individuals who had similar experiences. Before she had been raped she was an active missionary in her community. She conducted a children's story hour in her home where some fifty children attended. She collected food and shared with many persons in need. Until she could get back to them with her expanded ministry of helping those who had been raped or otherwise abused, she could not find healing. Today she runs her active children's ministry, shares food with the needy, and is actively engaged in fund raising for the building of a large church on the same island where she was raped. She is also rebuilding her business and enjoying an outstanding marital relationship.

The last time we spoke, she told me that the greatest reason for her healing lies in the hope she has that such ills as she suffered, will not be permitted in the earth made new. When she was raped, she said, "It felt like a snake had bitten me and poison had entered my body. It is good to know that the future will be nothing like this."[1]

Not all rape cases are mixed with such marvelous blessings, even in the midst of devastation. A large number of cases are unreported and the perpetrators are unindicted and unpunished. Victims are, therefore, left in the tragic realm of blame and shame. Even though, on a general basis, the case above might be thought to be typical, we can say it is non-typical, as all rape cases are. Each is personal and unique, and takes on a life of its own in the way each victim must relate to it. One's interest then is not to speak of rape in the typical sense, but to focus on the issue of rape and responsibility as the above case seems to portray.

Rape, blame and shame

Whenever a rape occurs a common way in which it is treated by society is to react with horror. At first there may be some sympathy for the victim. But then one commonly hears the questions that border on blame and shame. Why were they driving at night? Why did they stop to investigate when the road was blocked? Why were they out at such odd time? Why didn't they reverse the car and get out of there? Were they dressed provocatively? Why didn't they yell for help? The victims are often blamed and shamed. If the cases are reported, tried and sentences are sustained, the rapists spend little time in jail and are often returned into their communities to continue their criminal practices while their victims live with irreparable bruises. A few criminals are cured but since the majority of cases are unreported and victims tend to blame themselves, the crimes continue with perpetrators thinking that they will always get away.

One statistic about college rape victims says 42% of women who are raped tell no one about the assault, only 5% of all college women report to the police, and 5% seek help at a rape crisis center. Most of those who are raped, whether they report it or not, live with fear and powerful feelings of guilt and blame. Rape places its victims in positions of disempowerment.[2]

Rape is the ultimate expression of sex abuse, with 3 million cases reported each year in the U.S. alone. Add to this other sexual acts that are often passed off as legitimate, but in fact are violent sexual acts, and we have a pathetic picture of a chronic tragedy that plagues our society. Rape describes sexual activity without the consent of a social partner, in which case, rape might also occur inside of marriage. The majority of such cases go unreported because it involves one's word

against another's.   It is mostly a "hidden crime."   Nancy
Gibbs, writing in *Time*, captures the contrasting views of men
and women toward date rape.   Men "complain it is hard to
prevent a crime they can't define."   Women respond that date
rape as a crime "isn't taken seriously."   Men say "it is a
concept invented by women who like to tease but not take the
consequences."   Gibbs concludes that while men and women
argue among themselves about this "gray area" of sexual
relations without consensus, the heinousness of rape is not
being resolved either in the courts or on the campuses.[3]   In
most date rape cases, the tragedy shatters the promise of an
innocent evening with someone who supposedly can be trusted.
What starts out as pleasant conversation and enjoyable activities
ends in the violation of the rights and dignity of a woman (and
sometimes of a man, as Gibbs reports).

The pastor's attitude in the case cited might not have
been typical of the attitude of the sensitiveness that one can
expect of most pastors. I have ministered to rape victims, and
each time the crisis has compelled me to participate in the hurt
and the pain of the victims. Often I wished that my church had
better prepared me to deal with such critical moments. Even
among my congregants, I can't remember anyone ever talking
about rape in any constructive manner, except to note the event
as a "sign of the last days."

Rape of any kind, date rape, rape involving neighbors,
casual friends, strangers, or marital rape, violates the
personhood of the victim. When one adds unfair judgement on
victims as if they caused the crime by dressing inappropriately
or behaving in a "come hither manner," thus inviting the
violence perpetrated against them, adds to the ultimacy of the
tragedy.

Rape and Responsibility

Rape is the evidence of a judgement on our societal

norms and mores. We promote a culture that regards sexual activity more as an outlet of passion rather than as an expression of love. Movies and telecasts portray sex as a biological function indulged in casually without commitment. Even when speaking of freedom and equality of women, we still harbor the myth that women are subordinate to men, they being the weaker sex. Such social and gender-oriented myths contribute to manipulation of, and sexual violence, against women.

Rape, as an act of *violence* and *humiliation*, causes in the victim, an overwhelming fear for her very existence and an equally overwhelming sense of powerlessness and helplessness. This fear and helplessness are made even more threatening by the complex process of reporting a rape. Elaine Hilberman, chief editor of *The Rape Victim*, speaks of the trauma that a victim goes through when reporting her case. She may perceive the hospital and criminal justice system as insensitive, confusing, and alienating. Beyond that, the victim faces possible isolation even from family and friends. The crisis is not limited to the victim's person: the act of reporting makes the case public and puts the victim on public display.[4]

It seems to me that social organizations such as the Church, have a great part in treating in the most responsible way the issue of rape. What can the Church do? I suggest five main strategies.

1. *Provide a ministry of support.* Catching and punishing the rapist may be the objective of law enforcement, but that hardly restores the dignity and personhood of the victim. Rape victims need empathy and a sense of control over what has happened to them. The Church has the responsibility and the resources to assist victims in dealing with hospitals, law enforcement agencies, and perhaps the media. The Church need to help with healing the self-worth that victims of violent crimes frequently experience long after the event.

2. *Conduct educational programs in rape awareness.*
Given the society in which we live, the Church owes its
members an educational program that facilitates awareness of
rape and its personal, psychological, sociological, legal, and
moral consequences. Rape generates tremendous traumatic
reactions for victims and their families. The Church can help
guide them to available support systems.

Rape education should teach church members to take the
crime seriously. Rape is not a subject for jokes. The violation
of a person's most precious right is not to be taken lightly, nor
should it evoke condemnation of the victim. Rape awareness
programs should dispel certain myths perpetrated about rape,
such as:

a. The rapist is a sexually unfulfilled person,
    carried away by a sudden uncontrolled urge.
b. Rapists are sick.
c. Rapists are usually strangers.
d. Most rapes occur on the street, and so long as
    a woman stays home, she's safe.
e. Rapes occur because the victims ask to be
    raped by dressing seductively, walking
    provocatively, etc.
f. Only women with "bad" reputations are raped.
g. Most victims have been in trouble with the
    law in the past.
h. Only women in the lower social classes get
    raped.
j. Women can't be raped unless they want to be.
k. Rape is an adult crime; children are not
    involved.

3. *The Church should speak against all forms of sexual
exploitation.* Throughout Scripture, sexual relations are
portrayed as holy, ordained of God at the time of creation, not

to be indulged in frivolously, and certainly not to involve violent trampling of the rights and dignity of the marriage partner.

The seventh commandment is not simply a prohibition of adultery; it is a divine commission governing sexual relationships. Directives uplifting this model relationship abound in the Old Testament. A man who seduced a woman was required to marry her (see Deut. 22:13-29). To have sexual relations with an engaged or married woman was a capital offense (see Deut. 22:22, 24). Seducing an unengaged girl was a crime (see Ex.22:16, 17). Incest was prohibited (see Lev. 19:29). Many Old Testament stories illustrate the intense rage expressed against rapists (see Gen. 34; 2 Sam. 11:12-14; 13:14-33; 16; Judges. 20:5ff).

Although the New Testament does not speak specifically about rape, Christ's teaching on adultery defines for us the high road of sexual relationships. In the Sermon on the Mount, Jesus defined adultery not just as an act, but as a thought that precedes the act. "Anyone who looks at a woman lustfully," said Jesus, "has already committed adultery with her in his heart" (Matt. 5:28, NIV). This pronouncement affirms the highest value and dignity of a human being and precludes the passions and lust that motivate rape. Consider also how Jesus dealt with the woman caught in adultery (see John 8:2-11). He turned the table on the men who likely were responsible for her act. Jesus focused on the thoughts of the men toward that woman rather than on her actions or the accusation against her. As James Hurley points out: "It is not the presence of a woman, but the sinful thoughts of a man, which makes the situation dangerous."[5]

4. A church-conducted program of rape awareness should teach that *rape can happen even within a "Christian" marriage relationship*. A marriage in which one partner is submitted to abuse is a "violent marriage."[6] Spouses should be taught the rights and privileges of marital love and also be aware of its

responsibilities. Abuse, threats, and violence have no place in a Christian marriage.

5. Ministers and other leaders who are being prepared for church work should be asked to do serious introspection about themselves and their ability to lead congregations through rape and other crisis of this nature. Pastors need sensivity training in seminary education just as they receive education on how to preach.

6. Finally, the Church and all who understand the nature of rape should *pray for the healing of those who suffer bruises and abuses on life's road.*

ENDNOTES

1. This story told to me by a friend has been rather challenging for me to write. I thank her for permitting me to share it in this manuscript since it makes transparent the tragic feelings of even the best Christian when confronted by rape.

2. Daniel Macks, Internet page, extracted from Toby Simmon and Cathy Harris, Sex Without Consent: Peer Education Training for College and Universities.

3. Linda Marie Dellof, "Rape and Abortion in America," *Christian Century,* (Oct. 20, 1982), pp. 1037, 1038.

4. Elaine Hilderman, M.D., ed., *The Rape Victim,* (New York: Basic Books, Inc., 1976).

5. James B. Hurley, Man and Woman in Biblical Perspective (Grand Rapids: Zondervan, 1981), p. 109.

6. R. Emerson Dobash and Russsel Dobash, *Violence Against Wives,* (New York: The Free Press, 1979).

CHAPTER FIVE

SHE SAID, HE SAID: SEXUAL HARASSMENT AND THE TRUTH

Sex, lies and politics

The above title extracted from the October 21, 1991 *Time* magazine reflects on the most prominent issue in American political life which occurred in 1991, namely the Senate hearing for the confirmation of a judge to the supreme court. What started off as a well-ordered hearing soon became a "circus" in which senators seemed like gladiators, most seeking the "death" of Judge Clarence Thomas or Professor Anita Hill, alternatively and respectively.

Judge Clarence Thomas, the candidate for the confirmation was halfway through his hearing when some person with great political interest stated that a young professor, by the name of Anita Hill who had worked with the judge a decade before, could provide proof of being sexually harassed by the judge. From that moment on, the hearing lasted for 105 days with "accusations" and "denials" of one sort or the other. Each party in different ways, tried to sound more authentic than the other. One contributor in the magazine named above titled one commentary, "She said, He said."[1] From one news report to another, and from one commentary to another there were many perspectives on the case. But most dominating was the truth or falsehood of two characters who up until then, had been thought of as persons of the highest integrity in the land. Beyond the truth or falsehood of the characters, the topical issue of sexual harassment advanced from the case has a staple of American socio-political life.

Since the investigation of Judge Thomas and Anita Hill, other persons such as President Clinton, Senators, Congressmen, high ranking military leaders (especially cadets at the Citadel), sports figures, and many other professionals have been accused of sexual harassment. Of interest is the fact that what was treated as an issue for the courts is being made into soap opera. Moreover what had been thought of as occasional occurrences among a few misguided miscreants in a few offices, has been found to be endemic, epidemic and pandemic in homes, schools, job places, churches and most secular and sacred contexts where people come in contact with each other. The new realities have led states, professional and all working leaders to be educating their citizenry and clientele concerning sexual harassment and propriety. And though sexual harassment tops the list of issues that a company will educate its workers about today, harrassment seems to be continuing at a rapid pace. Truly something is radically sickening about our culture.

My interest in paying attention to the present culture of sexual harassment stems from the fact that I have seen enough tragedies of Christian professionals caught up in cases that have left some wounded persons, both women, (the usual accusers) and men (the usually accused) struggling to reclaim their lives. Thus how can we find resources to help Christians stay away from the game of lies, violence and cruelty brought on by the accusations and the excuses brought on by the charges of harassment. My further interest is not just to speak about how to deal with the lies, deception and defacement as the result of the charges of sexual harassment itself, but to speak of how Christians ought to behave with propriety in a sexually adversarial culture. The issue is not legal propriety as it is moral propriety, for it is morality that is creative of the good and leads away from abusiveness. Sexual morality, as I understand it, has to do with responsibility, integrity, fidelity, mutuality, dignity in relationship, and consent, not with sexual dominance, sexist practices, intimidation, rudeness, selfishness, sexual immorality, and sexual violence which have been made acceptable as a result of the sexual revolution of the 1960s and the last three decades of liberalized sexual codes. There is no question that sexual harassment has dominated the secret sins of human culture.   In any case, the Feminist and other movements of our time have made it more easily reportable and in one way or another, made it more possible as a sin of commission.   The issue here is not to suggest who is to be blamed so much as to offer biblical and practical suggestions as to how to transform sexual harassment into good instead of perpetuating it as one of the most tragic evils of our time.

Definitions of sexual harassment

Arising from a study of the whole issue, social scientists define sexual harassment as the use of power to coerce another into unwanted sexual relationships, initiating sexual behavior with another without appropriate invitation.   It might also involve consensual sexual behaviors with those with whom we relate in social and professional relationships, exploiting sexual conduct, betraying sexual boundaries, using inappropriate sexual gestures or seductive speech, having inappropriate physical contact and invading people's privacy. All aspects of the definitions depend upon particular conditions and contexts. Some actions which might not be considered sexual harassment for one person might be to another. And yet there is a general frame of behavior which may be beyond acceptability in every culture.   Although definitions might not be complete, it is comprehensive, and it can help us to sense the challenges of inappropriate relationships as they are presented in the conversations of the day. The interest is not so much to deal with sexual intercourse as it has to do with propriety in general sexual behavior. It has to do with whether one respects the dignity of another person, accepts that chastity is an appropriate ethical standard, and whether one is willing to use proper personal judgments in all situations. One must be willing to maintain (clear) boundaries thus avoiding dual relationships between employees, students, friends, business relationships, between friends and personal acquaintances. Any person who works in a profession or career in which he/she has to be in contact with the opposite sex will find a need for thinking seriously about what is appropriate sexual behavior. Just to say I am a moral or Christian person is not enough. To live the principles of Christian grace and to understand the nuances of a culture are both important in keeping a person from being charged in relation to harassment.

Sexual harassment and speaking the truth

A great challenge in sexual harassment is confessing the truth. In the context of public culture a charge of sexual harassment creates suspicion on every side. A gesture, a word, or an emphasis may be misunderstood. A constant question which we often hear is "Who is speaking the truth, the harassed or the harasser?" One only has to hope in every case that integrity will never be misunderstood. For Sissela Bok, "Lying . . . involves at least two people, a liar and someone who is lied to; . . . and the payoff configurations are rich in their possibilities . . . ."[3] Lying, as Bok sees it, affects people's choices, denies them the possibility of freedom, creates violence in relationships, destroys trust, manipulates situations, coerces persons to take inappropriate actions, brings harm to the self and others, undermines people's integrity, is used for intimidation, and much more that is negative to all of human life.[4] We hear a lot these days about he said and she said. It is therefore important that one ought to teach more on integrity.

The real issue for Christian life is to speak the truth and live the truth. Truth will always win. In the case of Joseph in

Egypt the revelation of truth took long, but in the end there was a magnificent vindication. The woman who accused the two members of the Dallas Cowboys of harassment then turned around and confessed to her misrepresentation of the truth, lost her own integrity, and called attention to the two men in ways that might leave them damaged for years to come. In the same trajectory of falsehoods many companies and organizations have lost noble workers and paid millions of dollars. Noble persons have lost their professional practice. And to the contrary, many persons who should have been treated with dignity when they called attention to their harassment have been dealt with as if they were the harassers. The veracity of their words have been treated with great disbelief and they are left to live with the double pain of being violated and disbelieved. One who remembers the pictures from the hearings of Judge Thomas and Professor Hill might still be challenged by the question of innocence, for until now no one is sure who spoke the truth. Was truth important in the case? So those who prosecuted the case thought. But the issue was not whether anyone was able to find the truth of that particular case. It was whether one political view was finding greater support than the other. The lack of proof might have set someone free, but the legacy of the investigation led to more suspicions of reported sexual harassment cases and therefore compromised the lives of many women. The case of President Clinton under investigation for sexual impropriety has not brought any betterment to the culture in which harassment occurs. The newspapers rightly report that "work environments have become the cesspool of lude and rude sexual jokes." As people battle with this political "hot potato," the late night shows continue to provide a spring board for the frivolous jokes which are taken to the work place. Persons working in their work environments who do not wish to participate in the sexual jokes are finding great difficulty in helping others to understand that their behaviors are considered harassment.

A young woman, well known to me and who suffers from a mentally handicapping condition, met me in a post office the other day while I was picking up my mail. She came up to me and recited what she called a Clinton sex joke then said, "Oh I love dirty jokes." I looked at her in shock while her mother who was close by, and apparently embarrassed the mother made sure I knew that it was the daughter who told the joke. But I felt badly for the mother and child since I know that the joke trivialized the truth. "What is truth?" and "Where is the truth?" are questions we need discernment to decipher in times of "virtual truth." In our contemporary culture our relationships are veiled by suspicion, because the truth is so difficult to be found.

Practical suggestions for dealing with sexual harassment

In dealing with sexual harassment a number of practical issues need to be considered.

a. The issue of seduction

One has to deal with facing the issue that often sexual harassment originates in the will for one person to seduce another. For Solomon, the sexual seducer is apt with persuasive words. With subtle comments and rude, cheap talk she/he can enchant the unwise. Even common kisses and hand shakes are used to the advantage of the harasser. A harasser works with crafty intent (see Prov 7). A Christian is different for he/she tries to be aware of symbolic gestures which might be misinterpreted. Any tenderness, any gaze, any affection, which might be interpreted as flirtation is avoided.

b. Facing one's own vulnerability

Another practical issue has to do with one's vulnerability. Individuals in certain professions need to understand their own vulnerability and they must therefore work with extra care at discretion. They ought to live with full awareness of shunning even the very appearance of evil. By this I mean that any condition that would knowingly allow for the accusation of sexual harassment should be avoided. In the book of Proverbs one is warned again and again about sexual seduction (cf. Prov 7). Following the the warnings there is an elaborate call for wisdom and prudence in all sexual practice (cf. Prov 8). Of interest to me is the fact that on a superficial reading of Proverbs, one finds that it is women who receive the heaviest burden as seductors. However, on closer reading one finds that men are at fault as well. In effect, one may not blame another for one's course of actions, but each must take responsibility for each ones self.

To the vulnerable I offer a series of recommendations that have been offered to pastors and priests by Richard M. Gula. He writes in his pastoral ethics that one needs to be aware of one's own and the other's vulnerability in regards to sexuality, especially in work relationships. His point is that where one holds greater power one holds greater responsibility for maintaining boundaries. One needs to learn how to avoid creating an offensive environment in the work place by unwelcome verbal, visual, physical contact of a sexual nature. One needs to learn how to avoid inappropriate sexual gestures. One needs to learn how to avoid seductive speech. One needs to learn how to avoid conflict of interests. One needs to learn how to avoid exchanging sex for favors. One needs to learn how to avoid inappropriate physical contact. For example, show prudent discretion in touching. Know when touching is appropriate. Calculate carefully when to touch or not to touch. This will demand attention to age, gender, race, ethnic background, emotional condition, and prior experience. Distinguish good touch from bad touch. Avoid initiating inappropriate sexual behavior and refuse invitations or consent to any such relationship. One should not satisfy one's need for intimacy, affection, attraction and affirmation inappropriately. Practice self discipline in regard to sexual relationships. When faced with circumstances that offer opportunity for accusations seek professional help.

c. Learning how to say "yes" and "no".

Another side of setting limits on behavior is knowing how to say "yes" and "no" to what one might feel appropriate or inappropriate behavior. Making people know when their actions make you feel uncomfortable is very important. When their words or actions seem inappropriate, all efforts should be made to allow them to understand your level of tolerance. I am stating that if our bodies as well as their private parts are treated as sacred, then the rules protecting them from profanization are to be observed. Who may approach them with intimacy, how they are approached and when they can be approached, are issues that one needs to settle. If the rules of sacredness are followed then people will know the limits of their conduct.

Sexual harassment and questions of justice

Saying the above does not suggest that one will not face some "devil" who will not seek to manipulate a situation until one is called to face conditions of sexual harassment. To such women and men, who feel themselves victims of a case, the story of Joseph in Genesis 39 can be rather assuring. Interestingly the story is given from a man's perspective, but it is quite fascinating even if it is inverted. It tells of how Mrs. Potipher worked through deception, manipulation and explicit sexual advances to get Joseph trapped in harassment. How Joseph's regard for God's laws, his self respect and deference for Mr. and Mrs. Potipher led him to refuse the advances. Although he took his flight, Mrs. Potipher was determined to undermine his character so she preserved the pieces of clothes she tore from Joseph clothing during his flight her advances. Upon the arrival of Mr. Potipher to his home, Mrs. Potipher gave a sincere and ingenious description of Joseph as a harasser. It was not hard for Mr. Potipher to believe his "trusted" wife. He therefore had the case reported to Pharaoh who ordered the trial which led to the conviction and imprisonment of Joseph. Joseph's redress only came years afterward when through divine providence, Joseph became the interpreter of the dream of a butler, a baker and one of Pharaoh's own dream. Such interpretation of dreams lead to Joseph's exoneration, release from prison and to administrative responsibilities.

The story does not suggest that every one who is falsely or truly victimized will receive justice in the world. But it does suggest that God is in charge of every life and will give it justice when it is victimized. We may be in situations in which the truth is distorted. We might watch and read stories of sexual harassment that leave us sick to the core. We might also feel that the present culture of suspicion is creating difficulty in trusted relationships. We might feel all of the challenges of a culture that is so sexually perverse. However, we cannot make the conditions of our culture define every aspect of our behavior. What must direct our lives today is the desire to transform the conditions of life. In speaking of morality in relation to sexual transformation, Henry Wieman, who gave up his commitment to traditional Christian faith, made a point that I think has some validity here. He said:

> . . . love between the sexes requires intricate and wide connections freely and openly established with all the rest of society giving access to the human heritage of beauty, truth, and devotion. The social

order, with its great body of institution and convention, is indispensable for this fulfillment of love. Therefore, solution of the problem is found not by repudiating the established order or by transgressing its demands but by changing it slowly so that it will permit the creation of contexts of value more widely and freely. When the nature of value and its source is understood, it should be possible in time to develop standards and a religion and social practices more hospitable to love's fulfillment. . .[5]

I am very much against the idea that transformative spiritual values can develop from the present social order in an autonomous way, as Wieman understood it. But I agree with him that we must find ways to trust each other. We cannot live with constant suspicion that someone is seeking to sexually harass us or we them. In effect, if we will understand how to use the power of love and the limits of love, we will not have to capitulate to some order of political correctness which might be spiritually or morally incorrect. In effect, if our dream of love is to be fulfilled we must participate in the struggle to transform a sexually suspicious culture.

ENDNOTES

1. *Time*, October 21, 1991
2. Sissela Bok, *Lying: Moral Choice in Public and Private Life*, New York: Vintage Books, Chapters 1,2.
3. *Ibid.*
4. *Ibid.*
5. Henry Wieman *(1995), The Source of Human Good*, (ed.) Terry Goodlove, Atlanta, GA., Scholars Press, pp. 240-241.

CHAPTER SIX

THE MORAL RESPONSE TO THE MOST POLITICIZED MORAL ISSUE OF TODAY

A personal crisis decision for a Christian

It was about 8:30 in the morning when the receptionist announced that someone would like to speak with me on the telephone. I picked up and quickly became aware that I was dealing with someone in a crisis. She said she had just entered the United States as an immigrant to join her husband. He'd been out of work for a few months and had just gotten another job. They were now trying to "set-up" themselves and bring the family together.

Two of their children were staying with their grandmother, while her husband and herself stayed in a sparsely furnished one bedroom apartment. She had just had the promise of getting a job when she began to feel very sick. Her feelings prompted a visit to the doctor and was subsequently told she was pregnant. She left the doctor's office in anger and despair. Upon returning home, she and her husband discussed the matter and made the decision that their only "alternative" was abortion. However, after her husband left for work the next morning she began to wonder if it were the right thing to do. That was why she called my office a day before, but no pastor was present to talk to her, so she was calling again "this morning."

Being a committed Christian she wanted to know what one of her pastors would have to say about her opting for an abortion. After listening to her story, I began to encourage her telling how my mother had ten of us and how happy she is that she did not abort any of us. We talked about what a privilege it was that her mother did not abort her. We also talked about the difficulty of making a decision when one is not willing to accept that God can help in the worst scenario of life. Then I asked, "So what are you going to do now?" and she said, "Pastor, I can see no way out. I have to." I felt the decision was made, but I tried to detain her a few more minutes by telling her that a few months before a relative of mine wrote me claiming that she was pregnant and had thought of an abortion. But her Christian faith helped her not to abort. So she went through with the pregnancy and had a handsome son. Now she is happy that she did not abort. Then I asked again, "Are you willing to go back to God and ask His help in making the right decision?" But she replied, "I will, however, I cannot see any other way but to abort." Hearing her last words I invited her to pray and said goodbye. I have not heard from her since. She did not give her name because she claimed that she was well known to her Christian community and would not want the people to know that she had aborted. But every time I think of her I say to myself here is a personal tragedy which is multiplied on a daily basis on a national scale. Abortion by choice, abortion as a means of birth control, and abortion for economic reasons, are dominating grounds for the large numbers of abortions in America today.

Abortion as a national political issue

Whoever the caller was, her case is typical. It fits a philosophy of life that has being adopted by a large number of persons today.[1] In fact, it is believed that there are some 4,320 such abortions each day, more than 15 million a year, more than 40 million since Roe V. Wade.[2] It is commonly acknowledged today that "Since 1973 the war on the unborn has produced as many causalities each year as have all the wars in U.S. history, from the Revolutionary War through Vietnam."[3] An unforgettable line from a newscaster a number of years ago states "Abortion has become one of the hottest issues of today." It is more than two decades since the lines have be drawn in the sand. Most persons today do not even know the historical context of Roe V. Wade, but they are caught up in the emotion of the debate and even take sides without question.

Nearly a decade ago Beverley Wildung Harrison noted that the abortion debate has moved outside the stream of normal political process and has pressed us into bitter social discord. The discord is multifaceted and deep, and all participants contend that human lives are at stake. In 1989 the Missouri Supreme Court reconsidered abortion and set forth a tremendous challenge to Roe V. Wade which has become a precedent for many other states since. Later, Pennsylvania passed a law that no abortions could take place after 20 weeks. In a few states, minors have been told that their decision to abort is dependent upon parental consent. The importance of the subject is seen when more than 273 groups are lobbying that the U.S. Congress put pressure on the U.S. Supreme Court to desist from removing any provisions of Roe V. Wade. At the same time many members of Congress are in a stand-off with the Supreme Court. Questions are being posed to the American public as to whether tax dollars should be used to pay for abortions generally and late term abortions specifically or even those resulting from rape and incest. The Congress is doing every thing it can to override a presidential veto on late term abortions. As presidential candidates state their positions regarding abortion, various pressure groups vow to make the debate a major plank of all election campaigns. Sometimes one has to ask whether the interest of the politicans is on the moral issue of abortion or whether they are only doing political posturing to see how they can get the most votes. The political spectrum presented is that to be a "hard core" Democrat, is to be "pro-choice," while to be a "hard core" Republican means to be "pro-life." That means, most politicians are having a certain religious ferver about an issue that concerns not only the unborn child but also everyone of us.[4]

The politics of convenience and the politics of conscience

It might not have been from personal feelings alone that ex-president, Ronald Reagan, published his 1984 book, *Abortion and the Conscience of the Nation*. It might have been with political interest. Whatever the interest, his preachy style left many individuals with the impression that he had a divine-social mandate to caution the nation on the moral basis of abortion. His thesis insisted upon the intrinsic worth and social value of all human life. It also mentioned the moral and ethical aspects of abortion, the law and abortion legislation, abortion as a social problem and the religious aspects of abortion. To date, his has been the most comprehensive effort of any sitting American President to speak against abortion. Whereas President Clinton makes mention of the issue, he leaves it to the Supreme Court, except on the issue of late term abortions.[5]

One area of profound anxiety today is not the public political debates so much as the fanaticism that surrounds the debates from all sides. Many persons opposed to legal abortion have moved far beyond the "art" of politics as persuasion to coercing those who seek to choose abortion. Thus, every day, the news media report acts of bombing abortion clinics, attacks upon persons who have wanted access to abortion facilities and a host of other tragedies. Entrances to abortion facilities have been blocked by angry pickets. Persons who have had abortions have been harassed on telephones, and many other coercive methods have been used. Though there are few arrests, the threat of violence over a volatile issue goes unchecked. Interestingly, it seems tragic that individual Catholics and Evangelicals and other Christian churches (most belong to the Religious Right) are contributing to the coercive side of the debate. And the question in many minds is whether the use of this kind of violence can be rationalized. When Cardinal Law of Boston called for a moratorium on clinic protests and for pro-lifers to find common ground with their pro-choice opponents, many Roman Catholics were wondering whether he meant for them to compromise. That is, did he mean for them to be indifferent? What about their traditional Catholic faith? What about the Pontifical statements on the sacredness of life?[6] Statement or no statement, what Cardinal Law acknowledged is that the abortion debate has reached beyond rationality.

The tragedy of violence has not been in the United States alone. On September 7, 1983, the Irish electorates decided by a two to one majority to amend their constitution to guarantee the right to life of an unborn child. Immediately, the issue brought a cleavage in religion and politics such as had not been apparent in Ireland. Irish society which had been characterized by authoritarianism, conformism and male domination, began to show that there were those who felt independent in thought and were willing to fight for their "rights." The same has been true of the Federal Republic of West Germany. Prior to the enactment of the fifth statutory to reform the Penal Law of June 18, 1974, West German law prohibited all abortions without exception. But it was not long before further reforms would change the strict laws and violence stalked the land.

Abortion in a culture of deception

The idea that we can call a horrific thing something else is of interest. But several terms used for abortion present it as less horrific than it really is. Some persons speak of it as "the extrification of the fetus from the womb." The idea here is that a fetus is not a real human being. Another idea is that because abortion is legal it is moral and ethical. But both ideas are false. The abortion debate needs to be placed in a context that is more than political and legal. On the memorable morning when I was telephoned by the young woman in my office, I figured my counsel would fall on deaf ears. I reflected that only a few persons in a crisis would pause to reason the moral basis of their actions. If people want to get rid of a fetus, for philosophical, political, social and economic reasons, they want to do it now, at any cost. But I pressed on to ask her why? Before technology had made abortion easy and secure, such persons might not attempt aborting for fear of death. Teenagers were not taught abortions as an option of contraception. They were often told to have the child and put it up for adoption. Now they are being told that abortion is the most potent form of contraception for nearly everyone. It is well documented that abortions took place before modern medicine, but not with such legal force and not as large percentage as we have it today. Today what we need to discuss is the struggle which church members have with a public moral system that controls moral thinking. In such a case, we need to focus on what it takes to face a world confused by falsehoods of morality.

In the Church the challenge becomes how to communicate principles and standards that will allow members to think through issues clearly, forthrightly, and with integrity. Integrity demands honesty, justice, and moral responsibility. This means, the will to save the life of an unborn child. To put into the same category abortion for saving a mother's life, abortion which deals with extraneous issues, abortion for rape, with abortion for contraception, is to confuse a very difficult moral issue. Many people on extreme sides of the abortion debate will never see how to separate out what has been so corrupted. My own view is that the falsehoods which exist in many of the contemporary perspectives between freedom and choice, between pro-life and pro-choice are never seen. Freedom and choice, prolife and prochoice are of equal importance to the Christian when positively defined. So, it is not whether one must exercise choice between life and choice, but it is whether one makes moral and responsibles choices. Proper choice, in the context of the abortion discussion begins with respect for life and one's moral obligation to God.

The question of sexual responsibility must be also pursued for most often an option for abortion is followed when there is failure to follow the principles which govern responsible sexual activity. The Christian cannot deal with things in a simplistic manner. What Christianity calls for is the determination of the divine will. The problem with our culture is that it frames choice and responsibility in abstractions so that one hardly contemplates its practical meaning. If most persons understood the consequences of abortion to their personal lives, and the society at large, they would think more carefully. In speaking about choice, the general emotional attitude of many "pro-choice" persons is that:

(1) A woman has a right over her body to do what she wills with it.
(2) A fetus is only a blob of tissue and not a person.
(3) A person has a right to be loved and cared for.
(4) Abortion is the surest way to take care of a mistake.
(5) Pregnancy is only a biological process.
(6) God understands that sometimes there is no other way out.

Much of the above is simplistic and deceptive. While some so-called reasons of the ideas may contain an element of truth, each is laced with deception.

Resisting the culture of deception

It is a rather interesting fact when one reviews Roe V. Wade and notes the deceptiveness that was involved. The young lady, Nancy McCorvey, who was used for the case under the name Jane Roe confessed to being complicitous to faking gang rape in order that the courts would hear her case.

Since the court did not deal with the case in time so that she could abort she carried her pregnancy to full term and put up her child for adoption. From the moment she gave away her child she began to struggle with herself. After years in defense of a pro-abortion stance, she began to work in abortion clinics and felt responsible for the number of daily abortions she saw taking place. In 1995 she was baptized by Flip Benham, the militant abortion leader of Operation Rescue. She has not actually given up her view of choice and thus argues for the possibility of legal abortion in the first trimester. Her positions may reflect convenience, but the reality of struggle is evident.

As far as using abortion as a means of contraception goes, a Christian should accept only one choice, God's choice of preserving life. That means sexual responsibility before abortion. Many means of contraception are available and the Christian may use many of them in a legitimate context. But those who engage in illicit sex should know that there are consequences that abortion cannot cure, but only exacerbate. Jeremiah has said that there are those whose eyes are only on dishonest gain, and therefore practice oppression, violence and shed innocent blood (Jerm 22:17).

The Church cannot control people's personal choices, for that is something God has offered to us in creation, but it must constantly warn against oppression. Gerald Winslow has correctly noted that Christian faith has fostered a high regard for personal freedom. He properly argues that we may encourage a person to seek the counsel of his/her faith community. And he justly cautions that one should not seek to coerce a person to make what one considers an acceptable decision in a matter so deeply personal. He is correct to say, "if anyone ever considers abortion, it indicates to some extent, a failure of the community."[7] On the other hand, we can speak about the recalcitrance of a culture that lives by individualism. A Newsweek article of August 21, 1995 reports Ms. Roe as saying that her stance is neither pro-choice or pro-life, but pro-

Norma.   My understanding is that Norma is consumed by individualism.   Individualism allows for all kinds of communal violence and this is what the Church needs to speak against. Let us teach communal responsibility for the innocent.

It seems to me that in the communities where we adopt divine obligation and moral responsibility as the foundational practice, we must remind members that abortion is not a simple question of choice, but a matter of communal responsibility. When we speak in this way we do not intend to be coercive, for Christian stewardship and community responsibility demand our clear understanding of freedom.   But they also demand guardianship over life.   We need to care and make people know it.   We must therefore teach people how to trust in God without being coercive or dogmatic.   We must say that using abortion as a means of contraception, even in the marriage context, is a very personal decision, yet it makes a profound comment on one's appreciation of life.   In all contexts one needs to consider the viability of life and protect it.   "When does life begin in the womb?"   "When does life end?"   These questions are not to be left to medical ethics alone, but are to spark our theological interest and our relationship to God.   The aim of our existence is to educate our consciences to the will of God.   To negate the educated conscience is to disobey the will of God.

The Christian response to life is not just to wrestle with areas of black and white, right and wrong, but with areas where the gray could lead to demonism.   Such questions as the importance of the life of the mother in late term are not to be left to chance, but are to be confronted and wrestled with until we understand that the life which is placed before the divine will will discern an answer.   Proper decisions are made after issues have been thought through clearly.   So one should not trivialize such profound moral issues.

Again, when we deal with abortion as contraceptive we must not act without moral obligation.   We need to name such abortion for what it is. It is a cover up for irresponsible sexual behavior.   The task of the Church is to offer correct information on the issue, speak against any immoral practice of the issue, and take the side of truth on the issue. How well has the Church led it's members to reflect on the sacredness of life is a great question. How well has it spoken of love and compassion in relation to the unborn is a question that the Church needs to keep to the fore. How well does the strong of the community protect the weak is a prominent issue.   In many ways we tend to depersonalize those we seek to destroy. We label them in dehumanizing ways and dispose of them with the greatest violence we can.   There is, therefore, need to ask the question which is being pressed so emotionally by the religious right, whether there is some connection between abortion, infanticide and genocide.   We need not minimalize these issues, because we are not of the right or left.   In the spiritual understanding, the sacredness of life must be judged by how we treat those at the margins as well as those who have their full potential of life. What do we do with those we think are in liminal space?   Do we name them as monstrous and valueless?

The above questions can be asked in many contexts, but the issue is fundamentally whether a person wishes to live in the will of God. To live according to such will is to avoid deception. It is to know that humanity is made in the image of God (Gen 1:27). The strongest argument that humanity should respect life, all of human life, is the fact that humanity is created in the image of God. Such an image does not begin outside the womb, but begins in it. I'm not arguing for any Platonic or Catholic doctrine here to suggest that there is a soul which enters into the body. My argument is otherwise, namely that any life at its beginning is potent with the divine image. Absolute perogative over human life is God's. Thus any diminuition of life is to be considered sinful, or rebellious to God.

The question about when life begins might only be answered by God. It is therefore a tragedy when we feel the kind of power we exert to take the life of the born or the life of the aged. While one group of persons in the contemporary world insists that a fetus is a viable person after 20-24 weeks, others insist that life actually begins at conception. We may have varying views of viability, but if our faith rests in God we will respect life.

The Bible explicitly states that:

Before I formed you in the womb, I knew you; and before you were born I consecrated you. I appointed you a prophet to the nations" (Jerm. 1:5) (R.S.V.). "Thou knowest me right well, my frame was not hidden from thee when I was being made in secret intricately wrought in the depths of the earth. (Psa. 139:15) (R.S.V.). "Thy hands fashioned and made me, and now thou dost turn about and destroy me." (Job 10:8) (R.S.V.).

No one therefore has a right to treat innocent life as if it is not of significance. We must always say it is a human tragedy that a person can do away with a pregnancy of 20 or 24 weeks and not feel any remorse. Followed to a logical conclusion abortion becomes the foundation for society to dispose of all those it thinks are on the margins of life.

Quite a few persons have argued that abortion parallels the ritual sacrificial practices in the worship of Molech, the goddess of the Ammorites. In the belly of this goddess a large fire was made and children were cast into the fire through a passage way in its genitalia. The people cheered as their babies were burned. Against such ungodliness, God warned Israel of the destruction that would come to the nation.

You shall not give any of your children to devote them
by fire to Molech, and so profane the name of your God
(Lev. 18:21).

One of Solomon's greatest sins was that he participated
in the ritual practice of child burning. He built an altar to
Molech and allowed Israelitish women to sacrifice their babies
to it (1 Kings 11:7).

From the above we can state that God expects our moral
choices to take on a seriousness of responsibility. Our actions
must lead us to protect all who are weaker than we are (Prov
3:31). We must think of the unborn as the innocent heritage
of the Lord (Psa 127). Those of us who believe in liberty and
seek to maintain it, need to recognize that issues like abortion
become an avenue which encourages governmental interference
into our personal faith. Paul Simmons, a leader in the
Southern Baptist Convention, said that the extensive political
involvement of various religious groups on both sides of the
abortion debate demonstrates the nature of abortion as an issue
of faith. Bitter acrimony and accusations show the potential for
even further loss of civility in the debate. There are also
threats to social stability. The battle has taken on a level of
hostility with shades of medieval religious wars. In short, the
abortion issue is testing our understanding of, and commitment
to religious liberty. In the same vein as Simmons, Robert
Maddox says that today's church state disputes are tomorrow's
courtroom battles.[8] We might need to suggest that while the
peoples of the world are fighting over false abortion
alternatives the people of God need to show their greatest
respect for life while affirming their freedom and choice.

Suppose Mary had an abortion.

I do not know how worthwhile one might think it is to
contemplate the question, but it has haunted me since it popped

into my mind a few years ago. The question is, "What would it mean for human salvation if Mary had had an abortion?" Mary, we know, faced the prospect of economic distress, social isolation, and condemnation of the most negative sort ever offered to a human being from the religious authorities. All kinds of emotions that impact a person faced with the issue of an unwanted and sometimes wanted pregnancy, turned in Mary's heart. She must have contemplated how she could have avoided any public censure. But her connection to God gave the positive perspective on her choice.

A person who hears the above question might be tempted to say there is only one Mary and only one Jesus Christ. Mary understood her role so well that she would not even contemplate abortion. She spoke with the angel of the Lord who instructed her on what her life was all about. One would hope that for every pregnancy all participants in the action that leads to the pregnancy could hear the voice of God. Then children would be taken more as the heritage of the Lord. Since procreation has been turned into an act of biology only, the value of who is responsible for the beginning and preservation of life seems to be minimized.

The argument concerning the possibility of Mary having an abortion can be turned upon its head by suggesting that the mother of Hitler would have done the world a favor if she had aborted Hitler and avoided the Holocaust. In any case, this latter argument disposes of the opportunity of salvation for Hitler and every other perpetrator of evil in the world. So the question persists, "What, if Mary had an abortion?" If the question does not permit an answer, it does allow us to reflect upon the tragic violence that led to the death of Jesus on the cross. All through life he was faced with violence. In the name of being in control, King Herod, under the guise of law and state security, killed the babies in Bethlehem. In the name of self-interest Judas handed Jesus over to the Sanhedrin (Mk 14:10, 2), who handed him over to Pilate (Mk 15:1, 10), who handed him over to the soldiers (Mk 15:15), who handed him over to death. This handing over was the ultimate of violence because it led the Savior of the world to the cross. Even though Pilate confessed in three emphatic statements, "I find no fault in this man for him to deserve death" (Lk 23:4, 15, 22), yet he handed Him over to be crucified.[9]

One can only trust that those of us who are Christians will associate the point, namely that the violence perpetuated against Jesus is consistent with the violence perpetuated against the living and the unborn. Every child is not Jesus, but what we do to the least of these affects Jesus. In fact, the birth and the death of Jesus should help us to speak with seriousness of the profound depth of moral responsibility confronting us to make life possible for those whom God creates in the world. So we need to be horrified when a would-be-mother takes a gun and shoots a child in its head while it arrives in the birthing passage, as we are horrified when two teenagers place their baby in a dumpster or in the toilet bowl. Alongside of each moral choice there needs to be some moral debate in our consciences as to how we stand in relation to God. No man or woman participating in this gruesome act should wash their hands with Pilate, stating "I am innocent of this person's blood." Pilate was irresponsible and so may we be.

Now while our legal and political systems might only recognize violence against life beyond the womb, God sees life as portentous and wills for its protection. Our culture might add violence to violence in the way it seeks to resolve the abortion crisis. But we cannot join in the oppressiveness of our culture and call it freedom. If we wish to live in faithfulness before God we must take care of those on the margins of life.

ENDNOTES

1. Rosalund P. Petchesky, *Abortion and Womens' Choice: The State, Sexuality, and Reproductive Freedom.* Boston MA. Northeastern University Press, 1984. cf. C. J. Postell, "Establishing Guidelines for Artificial Conception" II Tmal, 22 cf. Hyman Rodman, Betty Jarvis, Joy Walker, *The Abortion question*, New York: Columbia University Press, 1987. (N, 19860 93-95)
2. Thomas W. Hilgers, M.D. et.al. *New Perspectives on Abortion.* Fradrick, Md. University Press of America Inc., 1981. I would like to recommend as one of the most comprehensive on the abortion question. It covers the medical, legal, social, philosophical and the ethical aspects. It also gives a cultural perspective on how the problem is viewed. cf Marc Cooper, The Changing Landscape of Abortion," *Glamour* (Aug. 1995) 192-195, 251-252.
3. Roland Hegstad, Editorial, *Liberty*, vol. 84, No. 2, (March-April 1989).
4. Beverley Wildung Harrison, (1983) *Our Right to Choose: Toward a New Ethic of Abortion*, Boston, Beacon Press, p. XI. Eileen McDonagh, "Focusing on a woman's right to self-defense: A new argument on abortion" *The Chronicle of Higher Education* (Dec. 6, 1996) A 12.
5. A. Lake Randall, "The metaethical framework of antiabortion rhetoric," Signs, Sept 1986, Read the response to a letter sent to James Dobson by William Bennett "The right's new abortion right," *Harper Magazine*, (Jan 1996)
6. Todd Whitmore, "Common ground, no middle ground, crossing the pro-life, pro-choice divide," *Christian Century* (Jan 3-10, 1996) 10-12). cf. Schaeffer Frank, *Bad News For Modern Man: An Agenda For Christian Activism*, Westchester, III.: Crossway Books, 1984, p. 133. Daniel Callahan, "Abortion: Some Ethical Issues" in *Abortion Medicine and the Law* (eds.), J. Douglas Butler and Davis F. Walbert, New

York: Facts on File Publications, 1986, 341f.
7. Gerald Winslow, "Three perspectives on abortion: Perspective 3," *Adventist Review*, (Sept 25, 1986) 8-13.
8. Robert Maddox, ed. *Church and State* vol 42:10, (Nov 1989).
9. Leonardo Buff, (1979), *Jesus Christ Liberator: A Critical Christology for Our Time*, New York: Obris Books, 100-120.

CHAPTER SEVEN

ISSUES OF CONFESSION AND
THE COURAGE TO BE RESPONSIBLE

Public confessions and self-justification

Since Phil Donahue gave prominence to TV talk shows, public confessions of wrongs have become a part of American life. Many persons now go on TV to make public their deepest and most heinous deeds without much evident remorse. They tell of some abusiveness and brutality which have caused chaos to society. Jerry Springer, Ricky Lake, Gordon Elliott, Rolanda Watts, Jenny Jones and others are making a feast of getting people to manifest the darker sides of their souls. As hosts, they have profiled themselves as priests, pastors, prophets, and clinicians. They listen to the confessions and dole out their absolutions like some Grand Exorant, but often they argue that the peoples' actions are "natural". Some individuals are drawn with such compulsion to confess that they seem to manufacture fanciful sins. And the confessions are often so outrageous that one is led to wonder how in all the world can people find time and space to do such pathetic things. The morning, midday and evening news and every commentary seem to be drawn also into the culture of confession.

My point is to state in a concluding discussion, that while these new types of confessions are emerging today, there is little place for responsibility. What must be added to the confessions to make them responsible is repentance and reformation. While persons of the world will say "It is

"'Satan', or 'Society', which made me do it," Christian's must announce that Satan and Society can tempt us and corrupt us, but in the ultimate, all persons stand as responsible agents before God. The only path to transformation of the self and society is repentance. Feeding into the culture of ethical neutrality and self-justification is not acceptable for Christians. It was said of King Ahab of Israel, "He not only considered it trivial to commit the sins of Jeroboam son of Nebat, but he also married Jezebel, the daughter of the Sidonians" (1 Kings 16:31). Public confessors may glamorize sins and negligence, but such an attitude will not create a constructive moral direction.[1]

Dealing with our culture of irresponsibility

The questions we have dealt with in previous discussions lead us to the call to repentance. The prophet Ezekiel appealed to Israel thus, "Repent! Turn away from all your offenses; then sin will not be your downfall. Rid yourselves of all the offenses you have committed, and get a new heart and a new spirit. Why will you die O house of Israel?" (18:30-32). Without attempting to join any side of the public political debate as to whose is the most heinous sin in the nation, we can note that efforts at cover ups are many. And thus a prophetic call to repentance must be persistent. Abraham Heschel said many things of profound importance but one is very striking here, namely, that others may be satisfied with improvement, but the prophets insisted upon redemption.[2] Thus while accusations and trials take place, we need not pay so much attention to dramatized confession as much as we offer a call to repentance and redemption. Ted Peters is right in saying that by multiple games people have come to know how to place themselves "on the upper side of wrong." But this kind of staging does not bring about transformation of evil.

While some persons are portrayed as evil, others are being viewed as good. But the invention of lies that identify some with what is good while identifying others with what is evil does not solve a moral problem.[3] Writing in the same vein in *Theology Today* Quentin Schultze says:

> . . . the eclipse of sin has not reduced the amount of evil portrayed and reported in the popular media. It appears that evil, as a more publicly acceptable concept than sin, is doing more business than ever. News reporting and dramatic narratives are saturated with evil people and evil actions. These stories exist in everything from the nightly news to soap operas, prime-time drama, and movies. However, nearly all of this evil is disconnected from religious faith and any sense of transcendence. This secular concept reduces evil to morally wrong or bad actions easing harm or pain to other human beings, perhaps resulting in misfortune. In my judgment, if anthropologists unearthed, in the year 2220, the remains of current North American popular culture, they would find very little evidence for our culture's belief in sin, but they would simultaneously be overwhelmed at evidence for moralistic belief in evil.[4]

All of the above prompt me to suggest that the most blessed thing for individuals to do today is to acknowledge the heinousness of the past and seek a new future. This is the only way to deal with the heinous deeds among which I have named the sensual sins. Instead of seeking to explain away the wrongs of our sensual habits, our best course to responsibility is radical confession and the search for the divine forgiveness. Apart from this "How are we going to get to the future life in which people take full responsibility for their actions?" "How are we going to get beyond this self righteous predicament in which we find ourselves?" We all bear responsibility for the horrible things that we see in the world. We therefore have something to confess. We have something of which to repent. Only this confession and repentance will bring us joy and harmony.

Confession and repentance as general spiritual needs

Confession from the simplest perspective means the acknowledgement of a sin or a wrong. This does not say that one necessarily turns away from the sin or the wrong. To turn away one needs to combine confession with repentance. I speak of this combination because there are people who publicly boast of the evils that they do. I therefore, speak of responsible confession as "radical confession." Radical confession means turning away from the wrong and turning to the forgiving grace of God in Jesus Christ. "If we confess our sins, he is faithful and just to forgive our sins and to purify us from all unrighteousness" (1 Jn 1:9). To confess does not retain any corner of the life that is not available for the search by the Spirit of God. A full and radical confessional process is always comprehensive so that nothing is ever hidden from anyone. In "The Tell-Tale Heart", Edger Alan Poe describes a person who had murdered someone and hid the body in his basement. In taking the body to his own basement, he thought he would have been able to forget the crime. But he was so haunted by his conscience that he thought he could hear the heartbeat of his victim. Cold sweat washed him day after day until he realized that it was not the heartbeat of the dead body in his basement, but it was his own heart. The burden resting on him had helped him to recognize that he needed to come to terms with the reality of his heart, and the need for confession. It is a tragic thing when a person has a seared conscience, and cannot admit of sin in his/her heart. In this time when certain negative social practices have become acceptable as normative one has to be very careful of the lack of guilt.

Confession to oneself: Accepting personal responsibility

The authentic process of confession thus begins with self-examination, that is, hearing the heart in one's chest. A person thus stops hiding from himself/herself. Whatever the crime one must never be afraid to face it, then turn to the grace of God. An easier way than the way of personal acknowledgement is to make excuses, blame others or "pass the buck" as people like to say. We have spoken much of this practice of irresponsibility already, but we must speak of it again, because it shows in the pretenses of our confessions. The Psalmist spoke of his soul sickness when he said, "When I kept silent my bones wasted away . . . my strength sapped in the summer heat." However when he acknowledged his sin and did not cover up his iniquity he felt a peace with the Lord. Such forgiveness made him a "blessed" or "happy" man (see Psa 32).

Confessions are common and most persons crave participating in them, but the question remains "how much sincerity is involved in them" O. J. Roggee, quotes Publius Syrus of Rome (42 BCE) who wrote that "Confession of our faults is the next thing to innocence." Having studied many authors across the millenniums, Roggee notes that the biblical idea that sin in all of us is persistent, but he also notes how hard it is for people to engage in the call of God for sincere confessions.[5] In a reflection on confession he notes Mikail Zoshchenko's fascinating story, *The Wonderful Dog,* in which it is told how one Jeremiah Babkin sent for a bloodhound to make a search for a fur coat that was stolen. When the dog arrived with its keeper it was shown some footprints. It soon singled out a woman from the gathering crowd. The woman fell on her knees and confessed that she took five buckets of chicken feed, but that she knew nothing about the fur coat. The keeper then took the dog to the footprints, again. This time the dog singled out the head of the house committee. He too fell on his face and confessed that he had embezzled the water money. Next, the dog took hold of a young man. The young man immediately collapsed and admitted that he was a slacker: he should have been in the army but he had altered the date in his identity book and was living on the people. At this point Babkin handed the dog's keeper money and told him to take the bitch away. At this point, the dog went up to Babkin and smelled his goulashes. Babkin was embarrassed and finally confessed that he was a hooligan. The fur coat he was wearing belonged to his. He filched it from him. The people started to scatter. Nevertheless the dog grabbed two or three more. They all confessed. One lost government money at cards. Another threw an iron at his wife. The third made a statement that does not bear repetition. The yard was empty. The dog then went up to its keeper. The keeper paled, fell down before the dog, and admitted that he kept two thirds of the money that he got for the dog's food for himself. Here the story ended and no one is told what happened after.[6]   But the point was made. Many persons only confess under public pressure. The tragedy of such confessions is, of course, rather mechanical. They are coerced and leave one with the impression that most confessors are insincere.

We must therefore distinguish between the falsehood of confession which is on the fringe of religious consciousness, and that confession which is beyond that which is ethically neutral. While the former focuses on self security the latter focuses on transformation. In popular novels we find a falsehood of confession even under a title such as *True Confession* by Mary Bringle. However, what I intend is not a label which shows the glamorization of evil, but confession which seeks the cleansing of the Holy Spirit, for such a confession demands the criticism of the self and the searching of the heart. When David cried out "Search me oh God and know my heart, test me and know my thoughts, and see if there is any wicked way in me and lead me in the path everlasting (Psa 139:23, 23), he had a profound need for transformation.

Confession to God: Accepting moral responsibility

Here, one story which illustrates two opposite directions of confession as I speak of it, is told by Jesus of two men in the Jerusalem temple at worship (Luke 18:9-14). One of the men was a Pharisee, the other a Publican. Each prayed a prayer of confession, one with a mere desire for public approval, the other with a deep sense of personal commitment. The Pharisee, otherwise known as a "separatist" and legalist, followed more regulations than could be contained in any book. One example of the regulations commented on by Jesus was the washing of hands before meals. The hands had to be washed in a certain way, with one and one half eggshells of water. The water was poured on each hand then the hands were finally rubbed together with one fist first, then the other and then the hands were held up for the water to drain down upon the wrist and then run off. The washing was repeated a second time, then the hands were held down so the water could run down to the finger tips.

On one occasion, the Pharisees got into an argument with Jesus as to why his disciples ate with unwashed hands. Jesus answered that it was not that which went into the mouth that defiled the person, but it was what came out. Jesus was not encouraging unhealthy practices but he was showing disdain for pharisaical regulations. They had great disrespect for any one who rejected the regulations. It has been reported that one Pharisee said, "If there are only two righteous persons in the

world, I and my son are these two, if there is only one I am
he."[7]   In such a life, one could sense pious bigotry, arrogance,
and hypocrisy. In Luke's report, when the Pharisee stood to
pray, he raised his eyes toward heaven and said: "God, I thank
you that I am not like other people: thieves, rogues, adulterers,
or even like this tax collector. I fast twice a week; I give a
tenth of all my income" (Luke 18:11, 12). He was well
pleased with himself, having compared himself with other
human beings. He could therefore thank God that he came out
better than the thieves, rogues, and adulterers, or even the
unjust Publican. Then he reported to God that he fasted twice
per week, which meant that he went one more time than was
required. As a great act he gave a tithe of all he possessed.
The conclusion one comes to is, that the Pharisee was a self-
centered and self-righteous person who never felt a sense of
divine judgment upon himself. From his words all one could
hear was self- commendation. As the quintessential hypocrite
he thanked God that he was not as other people were. What
follows is the catalogue of his goodness. But the pretense of
his perfection is a reflection of his hardened conscience. He is
untouched by the Spirit of God for he has searched himself and
felt secure in his self-esteem, his self-assertion and self-
gratification. Abraham Heschel says that hardness of heart is
a condition which the person afflicted is unaware.   Not
knowing what ails him, he is unable to repent and recover.
However, when hardness is intensified from above,
responsibility is assured by God. He smites and he restores,
bringing about a revival of sensitivity.[8]

     On the opposite side of the Pharisee stands a sinner like
the Publican. He needs not be told of his rottenness. He
knows that he has participated in the rapacious Roman tax
collecting schemes and he places himself on the side of evil.
He knows that he is hated by the rich and by the peasants
alike. When he bows his head and smites upon his breast he

his only hope is that he is not rejected of God, so he cries: "Lord be merciful to me a sinner." Just a few penitent words, but he goes home justified because he trusts in the faithfulness of God. His confession is not prompted by pressure from without or fear of judgment, but it is prompted by his sense of the divine grace.

What is shown in the publican's prayer has a profound sense of respect for God. In his confession he only said "God be merciful to me." Then he threw himself on the faithfulness of God. In effect, the Publican understood that sincerity before God was worth more than reputation. He understood that no sinner could truly stand in the presence of a holy God without acknowledging the reality of his guilt. As Heschel says, "When all pretensions are abandoned one begins to feel the burden of guilt.[9]

The Pharisee's confession	The Publican's confession
He ignores his sin before God.	He feels the wretchedness of himself as a sinner.
He feels a great sense of merit. God owes him something.	He acknowledges that he has no merit before God.
He engages in the illusion of confession but suppresses the truth of his life.	He is truly vulnerable and takes responsibility for his actions
He is full of self-praise	He knows he has nothing for self praise
He judges others concerning their sinfulness	He feels self abhorrent and seeks to expunge the evil of his ways

The issues that I seek to challenge have to do with self-righteousness and complacency. These are issues that are at the core of the destruction of our contemporary culture. And both issues affect religious communities. My point is that when we accept Christ we must find a new way to relate to our self-indulgent culture. Christian responsibility is not determined by culture. It is determined by the life lived in righteousness. In making a call for the practice of love, justice, and righteousness, Abraham Heschel has said:

> Sacred fire is burning on the alters in many lands.
> Animals are being offered to the glory of the gods.
> Priests burn incense, songs of solemn assemblies fill
> the air. Pilgrims are on the roads, pageantries in
> the sacred places. The atmosphere is thick with
> sanctity. In Israel, too, sacrifice is an essential act
> of worship. It is the experience of giving oneself
> vicariously to God and being received by Him.
> And yet, the pre-exilic prophets uttered violent
> attacks on sacrifices . . . while (for example)
> Samuel stressed the primacy of obedience over
> sacrifice, Amos and the prophets who followed
> stressed the primacy of morality over sacrifice, but
> even proclaimed that the worth of worship, far from
> being absolute, is contingent upon moral living, and
> when immorality prevails, worship is detestable.
> Questioning man's right to worship through
> offerings and songs, they maintained that the
> primary way to serving God is through love, justice
> and righteousness.[10]

True innocence is generated by the righteousness of God

The point which I am emphasizing is this.   Any

innocence with which we are declared is not of human work or deception, but it is that which is given by the righteousness of Christ. To keep our vows of faithfulness to Christ is therefore the greatest thing for which we are to strive. One approach to sin is to seek to hide the wrong and discount the sin, and this is not open to Christians. To generalize sin, to gloss over it, to excuse it, to down-play its tragic power, and call it something else, is the approach of the forces of demonism. The Christian approach to sin is to see it as malevolent and reject it. While the Pharisee thinks he has no sin, the Publican owns his sin and seeks to be forgiven of it. The Publican says, "It is my sin." "I am a man of guilt." "I am responsible." "I have broken the relationship between me and God, me and my neighbor, me and my community at large." "I deserve punishment." "How can my relationship be righted?" This is the frank admission we fail to require in much of our Christian culture. Even while I fear being misunderstood for calling for a renewal of the sense of guilt, I fear that we have come too far into "the easy conscience" of modernity. When we abort the unborn, abuse the innocent and destroy the lives of countless persons in our land, we seem not to feel any responsibility. We simply say "that is my private business." But it is my contention that the burden of a sickened conscience should urge us to find God instead of driving us to find our own solutions.

As true confessors we must understand that we do not need to be going on public radio or TV to acknowledge our sins. Coerced confessions are insincere confessions. What we need is to face our God. The most profound reality of life is that we stand before God and God alone. One needs to speak to God, silently and sincerely, specifically and generally, personally and communally, for in these ways we can deal comprehensively with our actions and state of being. David sets the example when he said:

> Against you, you only have I sinned, and done that
> which is evil in your sight, so that you are justified
> in your sentence and blameless in your judgement
> (Psa 52:4). Then I acknowledged my sin to you,
> and I did not hide my iniquity; I said "I will confess
> my transgressions to the Lord," and you forgave the
> guilt of my sin. Therefore let all who are faithful
> offer prayer to you, at a time of distress, the rush
> of mighty waters shall reach them. (Psa 32: 5-6).

The fundamental action in all confessions then is to
confess our failures to the God of the universe, but this is only
a beginning.

Confession to those wronged - Community responsibility

There is a follow up to one's confession to God, namely
the confession to one's neighbors. This places the emphasis on
the horizontal side of religion. If the vertical is to work
effectively, we must also deal with the horizontal. All of us
have persons whom we have offended: our family members,
children, spouses, our friends, our colleagues at work, our
leaders, and those who follow us. All of us have participated
in sins of oppression and suppression: racism, sexism, classism
or some other actions of injustice. The catalog is great and it
must not be pressed as if to force an admission, but it seems
hard that any one should try to be pharisaical about innocence
here, for Scripture says:

> So when you are offering your gift at the altar, if
> you remember that your brother or sister has
> something against you, leave your gift there before
> the altar and go; first be reconciled to your brother
> or sister, and then come and offer your gift (Matt

5:23, 24).

And if the same person sins against you seven times a day, and turns back to you seven times and says, "I repent," you must forgive (Lk 17:4).

Therefore, confess your sins to one another, and pray for one another, so that you may be healed (James 5:16).

Confession to a spiritual advisor - Overcoming autonomy

The concept of confession to God and neighbor should seem comprehensive enough, but because of the need for reconciliation in difficult situations we need to take confession to the level where it is assisted by a spiritual guide. This has nothing to do with a particular mechanistic view of guidance as it is used in the Roman Catholic tradition. But from the understanding of a spiritual support, I feel there is need to commend it. Some persons have such burden of conscience for their actions against society that they cannot carry their burdens by themselves. It is good advice then to say that a person should seek one who has maturity in the things of God and confess. The point is to find someone who can help a person so burdened to gain a proper perspective on the self and the ways of dealing with those wronged. When looking for a spiritual help, do not seek a person to put you down, but one who knows what it means to build up another person. I think here of David who admitted to Nathan, "I have sinned against the Lord." Then Nathan said to David, "Now the Lord has put away your sin; you shall not die. Nevertheless because by this deed you utterly scorned the Lord, the child that is born to you shall die. Then Nathan went to his home" (2 Sam 12:13 - 15). This was profoundly assuring. The point is that in our lives there is a time and place to learn vulnerability. That vulnerability however, must be confronted by respect and confidentiality. The one who hears the confessor is to be filled with the dignity of love for the public protection of the other person.

Confession to an intimate community - A way of succoring another

There is a time and place for confession to an intimate as there is place for confession to a larger public community. I will deal with the latter following. Here I simply seek to note the scriptural principle as stated in Matthew that when a member of a church community is in error such a person should be confronted by one person, and if such a one will not listen he/she should be confronted by a few community members. Still if he/she refuses to listen he/she should be brought before the entire community and there the offender should be treated as a Gentile or a tax collector (Matt 18:17). The confessional practice was very well known in the New Testament Church and James makes reference to it when he says "Confess your faults to each other and pray for each other that you may be healed" (James 5:16). The Johannine churches were as typical. Those who did not see their need for confession were called "liars" and seditionists (cf 1 Jn 1). The intent of the confession was to build the fellowship. This kind of confession was not intended to embarrass anyone but to create reconciliation. This kind of confession is not so popular today, but one might advise that where there is public sin and public scandal, the Church of God must revert to the New Testament pattern of confession and remove guilt from the presence of God's people. The purpose of this confession is based upon the reality that all of us are sinners. There needs not be any self righteous attitude, but a recognition that it is only by the grace of Christ that one can be released from sin.

When we are told to pray for those who are overtaken in a fault, it should call forth our most profound emotion.

Corporate confession and corporate sin

There is also such a thing as cooperate confession. In the midst of a presidential investigation and an impeachment vote, it is quite transparent when we speak of it. For although many persons are tending to focus on the one sinner there is a great truth that all have sinned and come short. When a leader betrays public trust, the whole community cannot just hide behind a leader's sin. Though the community cannot be complicitous with the leader's sin, it makes trivializes confession when it turns confession into coercion. There can be much tragedy when a community is so focused on the act of some leader that it does not see its own sin in participating in the false ideologies or legalistic practices it promotes. History has taught us that the downfall of nations has come as a result of hatred and pride in as much as it has come through the arrogance of a leader. But let us suspend particular questions and say that when leaders with political pretense call for public confessions in order to defeat one political party over against another, one has to wonder what is the definition of responsibility and morality. Cooperate sins are not the sins of one or the sins of a few, but they are often the complicitous actions of the many. The many must therefore resist the temptations of moralization and turn to God as the only forgiver of all. We therefore, can learn a great lesson from Daniel in Babylon, as he reflected on the sins of his people. He laid emphasis on the following phrases: "We have sinned," "we have committed iniquity," "we have rebelled" (Dan 9).

Confession and repentance

In all of the prophets there is a constant call for

confession and repentance. Joel says: "Blow the trumpet in Zion, sanctify a fast, call a solemn assembly," so that the nation might repent of its sins (Joel 2:15). The prophet Jeremiah charges the nation with deceit, violence, adultery and gross idolatry, then he calls, "Return faithless Israel . . . Only acknowledge your guilt . . ." (3:12-13). "Return faithless people . . . If you will return, O Israel, return to me," declares the Lord. "If you put your detestable idols out of my sight and no longer go astray, and if in a truthful, just and righteous way you swear, as surely as the Lord lives, then the nations will be blessed by him and they will glorify him." (Jerm 3:14; 4:1,2). Prophetic movements understand this need for calling for atonement. My major reason for writing these reflections is to create a prophetic consciousness so that we can allow our voices to be heard more clearly in the call to genuine atonement. The call is for greater responsibility, even as we put out our garbage before our children in the discussions of sexual scandals and other news of sensuality. When all of public media is turned into smut, it is time for all to call for responsibility again.

When President Abraham Lincoln proclaimed the last Thursday of September as a day of contrition, confession and prayer, in 1861, he did it because the Civil War had become a national tragedy for America. Some historians have seen President Lincoln as a national prophet. I do not seek to classify him here except to state that in he knew how to confront a national tragedy. We must therefore ask our communities, even our communities of faith, to become contrite and confess our wrongs. Our victory over deceit and violence will not come with the kind of hand washing that we have seen in Pilate and the Macbeths. No! It will only come when we own our sins and turn to God to help us build our to a new future.

In speaking of confession we have noted two basic issues.

The one focused on the confession of our faith and the other on the confession of our sins. These two things bring us to the ultimate issue of life, namely the reality that each person stands before God as moral agent. As moral agents we follow the path to transformation, that is what Rienhold Neibuhr used to call the "courage to change." In effect, we need to change from foolish pride, self-deception, self-assertiveness and self-righteousness, for these together are the sins that lead to the idolatrous worship of our desires.

In the whole context of sexual ethics on which I have focused, the transformation for which I call pays attention to gaining mastery over our bodies and our spiritual lives. When we see Christ we can arise like the prodigal and ask for mercy. Ellen White rightly says that, "In him [Christ] is our hope, our justification and our righteousness."[11] In the book of Proverbs we are told that "All one's ways may be pure in one's own eyes, but the Lord weighs the spirit." (Prov 16:2 NRSV). If we are to live with integrity and responsibility we must therefore be subject to Christ.

In the judgment of our consciences Paul asks a critical question, namely: "Who will bring any charge against God's elect?" (Rom 8:33) He then answers: "It is God who justifies. Who is to condemn? It is Christ Jesus, who died, yes, who was raised, who is at the right hand of God, who indeed intercedes for us." (Rom 8:34). Isaiah makes the same point concerning the divine righteousness and expectation concerning the judgment of conscience when he says:

> Your hands are full of blood; wash and make yourselves clean. Take your evil deeds out of my sight! Stop doing wrong, learn to do right! Seek justice, encourage the oppressed. Defend the cause of the fatherless, plead the case of the widow. "Come now, let us reason together, says the Lord. Though your sins are like scarlet, they shall be as

white as snow; though they are red as crimson, they
shall be like wool. If you are willing and obedient,
you will eat the best from the land; but if you resist
and rebel, you will be devoured by the sword."
For the mouth of the Lord has spoken . . . (Isa
1:15 LP - 20).

My conclusion is that even a Pilate, a Judas or a Macbeth
could receive the divine approbation if they were to confess
and repent of their sins.   In the historical context, each
character waited and tried to wash their hands and walked away
as if they were innocent. They faked the politics of innocence
and ended up with moral confusion.   They lived out the
essence of a few lines that I wrote some years ago, namely:

> Where politics reigns, words
> of confession are rarely sincere.
> Where politics reigns, the language of
> forgiveness is little thought of.
> Where politics reigns, few persons
> want to be answerable.
> Where politics reigns, integrity
> will often be missing.
> Where politics reigns, humility
> will often be forgotten.
> So how might we clean up politics?
> Clean up our hearts.

When we wash our hearts of sin, we can begin to live our
lives again.   Here then, we recognize that the politics of
innocence is not the washing of one's hands or the washing of
one's feet. Neither is it the washing of the body or bathing in
expensive perfumes. The politics of innocence is the washing
of the life as Peter recognized it when he cried out "Lord, not

my feet only but my head as well!" (Jn 13:9). If we will overcome the irresponsibility which drives us to deception, we must confront ourselves and pray, "Lord strengthen our minds against the seductive temptations of our time." That is, we must ask God to hold our passions and appetites in subjection to his will. Then, we must consecrate ourselves to live by the principles of grace that make us the kinds of persons God wants us to be. And we must pledge not to worship the way of desire and seek the Holy Spirit's aide in our discernment. For only when we have a profound commitment to the holiness of the divine that we can live with integrity, honesty and responsibility.   In effect, to be innocent demands a thoroughness of grace. And in this way we can say, "We got the blood off our hands," and "We are innocent of this person's blood."

ENDNOTES

1. Robert Wright, "Science and Original Sin," *Time*, (October 28, 1996) 76-77.

2. Abraham Heschel (1962), The prophets, New York: Harper & Row, 181.

3. Ted Peters (1994), *Sin: Radical Evil in Soul and Society*, Grand Rapids, MI.

4. Quentin J Schultze, "Civil Sin: Evil and Purgation in the Media" *Theology Today*, (April, 1991), 229-242.

5. O. John Roggee (1959), *Why Men Confess*, New York: Thomas Nelson and Sons.

6. O. John Roggee, précis of Mikail Zoshchenko, *The Wonderful Dog*, cited above, 172.

7. See William Barclay (1970), *And Jesus Said*, Philadelphia: The Westminster Press, 100.

8. Abraham Heschel (1962), *The Prophets*, New York: Harper & Row, 181.

9. *Ibid.*, 193
10. *Ibid.*, 195.
11. Ellen White (1958), *Patriarchs and Prophets*, Boise, IO.: Pacific Press Publishing Association, 306-308.

ORDER FORM

To receive additional copies of *The Politics of Innocence*, mail your prepaid order to:

Unity Research Institute
P.O. Box 554
South Lancaster, MA 01561

Name_____

Address_____

State_____Zip_____

Phone_____

Amount Enclosed_____$_____